The Stupidity Epidemic

Joel Best

Critics often warn that American schools are failing; that our students are ill-prepared for the challenges the future holds, and may even be "the dumbest generation." We can think of these claims as warning about a Stupidity Epidemic. This essay begins by tracing the history of the idea that American students, teachers, and schools are somehow getting worse; the record shows that critics have been issuing such warnings for more than 150 years. It then examines four sets of data that speak to whether educational deterioration is taking place. The essay then turns to exploring several reasons why belief in educational decline is so common, and concludes by suggesting some more useful ways to think about educational problems.

Joel Best is Professor of Sociology and Criminal Justice at the University of Delaware. His work focuses on deviance and the sociology of social problems. His most recent books are *Social Problems* (2008), *Stat-Spotting: A Field Guide to Identifying Dubious Data* (2008), and *Everyone's a Winner: Life in Our Congratulatory Culture* (2011).

Framing 21st Century Social Issues

The goal of this new, unique Series is to offer readable, teachable "thinking frames" on today's social problems and social issues by leading scholars. These are available for view on http://routledge.custom gateway.com/routledge-social-issues.html.

For instructors teaching a wide range of courses in the social sciences, the Routledge *Social Issues Collection* now offers the best of both worlds: originally written short texts that provide "overviews" to important social issues *as well as* teachable excerpts from larger works previously published by Routledge and other presses.

As an instructor, click to the website to view the library and decide how to build your custom anthology and which thinking frames to assign. Students can choose to receive the assigned materials in print and/or electronic formats at an affordable price.

Body Problems
Running and Living Long in a Fast-Food
Society
Ben Agger

Sex, Drugs, and Death
Addressing Youth Problems in American
Society
Tammy Anderson

The Stupidity Epidemic
Worrying About Students, Schools, and
America's Future
Joel Best

Empire Versus Democracy
The Triumph of Corporate and Military
Power
Carl Boggs

Contentious Identities
Ethnic, Religious, and Nationalist Conflicts in
Today's World
Daniel Chirot

The Future of Higher Education
Dan Clawson and Max Page

Waste and Consumption
Capitalism, the Environment, and the Life of
Things
Simonetta Falasca-Zamponi

Rapid Climate Change
Causes, Consequences, and Solutions
Scott G. McNall

The Problem of Emotions in Societies
Jonathan H. Turner

Outsourcing the Womb
Race, Class, and Gestational Surrogacy in a
Global Market
France Winddance Twine

Changing Times for Black Professionals
Adia Harvey Wingfield

Why Nations Go to War
A Sociology of Military Conflict
Mark Worrell

The Stupidity Epidemic

Worrying About Students, Schools, and America's Future

Joel Best

University of Delaware

Routledge
Taylor & Francis Group

NEW YORK AND LONDON

First published 2011
by Routledge
270 Madison Avenue, New York, NY 10016

Simultaneously published in the UK
by Routledge
2 Park Square, Milton Park, Abingdon, Oxon OX14 4RN

Routledge is an imprint of the Taylor & Francis Group, an informa business

© 2011 Taylor & Francis

The right of Joel Best to be identified as the author of this work has been asserted by him in accordance with sections 77 and 78 of the Copyright, Designs and Patents Act 1988.

Typeset in Garamond and Gill Sans by EvS Communication Networx, Inc.

Library of Congress Cataloging in Publication Data
Best, Joel.
The stupidity epidemic : worrying about students, schools, and America's future / Joel Best.
p. cm. — (Framing 21st century social issues)
1. Educational accountability—United States. 2. Educational productivity—United States. 3. Education—Political aspects—United States. I. Title.
LB2806.22.B48 2011
370.973—dc22
2010027986

ISBN13: 978-0-415-89209-4 (pbk)
ISBN13: 978-0-203-83421-3 (ebk)

Contents

Series Foreword

The world in the early 21st century is beset with problems—a troubled economy, global warming, oil spills, religious and national conflict, poverty, HIV, health problems associated with sedentary lifestyles. Virtually no nation is exempt, and everyone, even in affluent countries, feels the impact of these global issues.

Since its inception in the 19th century, sociology has been the academic discipline dedicated to analyzing social problems. It is still so today. Sociologists offer not only diagnoses; they glimpse solutions, which they then offer to policy makers and citizens who work for a better world. Sociology played a major role in the civil rights movement during the 1960s in helping us to understand racial inequalities and prejudice, and it can play a major role today as we grapple with old and new issues.

This series builds on the giants of sociology, such as Weber, Durkheim, Marx, Parsons, Mills. It uses their frames, and newer ones, to focus on particular issues of contemporary concern. These books are about the nuts and bolts of social problems, but they are equally about the frames through which we analyze these problems. It is clear by now that there is no single correct way to view the world, but only paradigms, models, which function as lenses through which we peer. For example, in analyzing oil spills and environmental pollution, we can use a frame that views such outcomes as unfortunate results of a reasonable effort to harvest fossil fuels. "Drill, baby, drill" sometimes involves certain costs as pipelines rupture and oils spews forth. Or we could analyze these environmental crises as inevitable outcomes of our effort to dominate nature in the interest of profit. The first frame would solve oil spills with better environmental protection measures and clean-ups, while the second frame would attempt to prevent them altogether, perhaps shifting away from the use of petroleum and natural gas and toward alternative energies that are "green."

These books introduce various frames such as these for viewing social problems. They also highlight debates between social scientists who frame problems differently. The books suggest solutions, both on the macro and micro levels. That is, they suggest what new policies might entail, and they also identify ways in which people, from the ground level, can work toward a better world, changing themselves and their lives and families and providing models of change for others.

Readers do not need an extensive background in academic sociology to benefit from these books. Each book is student-friendly in that we provide glossaries of terms for the uninitiated that are keyed to bolded terms in the text. Each chapter ends with questions for further thought and discussion. The level of each book is accessible to undergraduate students, even as these books offer sophisticated and innovative analyses.

Joel Best examines a topic that will fascinate all young people, and their parents! He asks whether we are getting more stupid and whether education and culture are failing us. Is stupidity an epidemic? Reality television, Wikipedia, cell phones, video games would suggest a decline of discourse and intellectual seriousness. Best explores whether these trends suggest social stupidity, or whether we are exaggerating the impact of undeniable trends such as increasingly reliance on rapid information and communication technologies. His book is an excellent test of whether people tend to believe that the sky is always falling, even where careful evidence suggests otherwise! One of the main implications of his study is that our arguments need to be evidence-based.

Preface

I was a suburban child in the 1950s. Although many commentators imagine this was a bland place in a bland decade, I recall it as a time when people worried about a lot of social problems–communism, of course, but also organized crime, juvenile delinquency, divorce, the impacts of television and rock and roll, and the failure of American schools to prepare kids for the future. As a child, I read pretty much anything within reach, and I was fascinated by all of the alarming news. As a sociologist, I've remained interested in how and why social problems come to public attention.

One advantage of growing older is that you have a lot of memories. In my case, I can remember a lot of frightening claims about social problems–about the worrisome emergence of beatniks, hippies, punks, and slackers; about the epidemic spread of heroin, marijuana, and all sorts of other frightening drugs; and the list goes on and on. Each of these problems was presented as new and very serious, as something that society couldn't afford to ignore. And, in retrospect, many of those worries now seem overblown, even silly–particularly compared with today's problems, which we understand to be new and very serious.

I wrote this book because I thought claims about the failures of American education offer a way to think about the process by which social problems attract public attention. There are plenty of people worrying about the failures of today's schools. For the most part, those people have forgotten the generations of earlier commentators who had very similar concerns and, for the most part, they also ignore the readily available evidence that shows their fears are misplaced.

In my view, thinking about Americans' worries about schools can not only help us better understand educational issues, it also offers a model for thinking about all sorts of alarming claims about social problems.

Acknowledgments

Tammy Anderson, Nancy Berns, Jeff Davidson, Robert Hampel, Kathe Lowney, and Dave Schweingruder made helpful comments on a draft of this paper. I also want to thank Rhys Williams and Diane Pike for giving me opportunities to organize and develop these ideas.

I: Our Doubts about America's Schools

~~~✤~~~

Y ou've seen the headlines: "Americans Falter on Geography Test" (*New York Times* 1988); "Survey Finds Many Have Poor Grasp of Basic Economics" (Walsh 2005); "Scientific Savvy? In U.S., Not Much" (Dean 2005); "College Students Struggle on History Test" (Briggs 2007); "U.S. Doesn't Know Civics" (Healy 2008). Someone sponsors a survey designed to measure "geographic **literacy**" or "economic literacy" or whatever; they hold a press conference highlighting the generally dismal results, and the news media marvel at the simple facts Americans don't seem to know.

For instance, the 2006 Geographic Literacy Study, sponsored by the National Geographic Society and conducted by the Roper polling organization, surveyed 510 young Americans aged 18 to 24. It found: "Six in ten (63%) cannot find Iraq on a map of the Middle East, despite near-constant news coverage since the U.S. invasion of March 2003," and—the intense coverage of Hurricane Katrina and its aftermath notwithstanding—only two-thirds could locate Louisiana on a U.S. map (National Geographic–Roper Public Affairs 2006: 6, 8). (Actually, that Katrina coverage may have helped—only 43 percent could spot Ohio.) The study's bottom line: "Most young adults between the ages of 18 and 24 demonstrate a limited understanding of the world beyond their country's borders, and they place insufficient importance on the basic geographic skills that might enhance their knowledge" (National Geographic–Roper Public Affairs 2006: 6).

Such stories highlighting Americans' ignorance have become routine. The same basic theme of national stupidity runs through popular culture. In 2007, the Fox television network launched a new game show, "Are You Smarter Than A 5th Grader?," in which adult contestants could compete for a million-dollar prize by answering a series of questions based on the fifth-grade curriculum. The vast majority of contestants eventually bowed out, and were required to acknowledge that, indeed, they weren't smarter than a fifth-grader. "The Tonight Show with Jay Leno" featured "Jaywalking," a recurring segment in which Leno videotaped passersby on the street incorrectly answering simple questions (such as "What color is the White House?"). Bookstores display an array of serious nonfiction titles denouncing our widespread stupidity, such as *The Dumbest Generation* (Bauerlein 2008), *Dumbing Us Down* (Gatto 2002), *The*

Knowledge Deficit (Hirsch 2006), and *Just How Stupid Are We?* (Shenkman 2008). On nearby shelves, guidebooks in two popular series, *The Complete Idiot's Guide to* _____ and _____ *for Dummies*, suggest a widespread, cheerful willingness to acknowledge our ignorance.

It is easy to link these claims about widespread ignorance to critiques of American education. If we're dumb, it must be because schools aren't doing their job teaching us what we need to know. And clearly we're worried about our schools. When the Gallup Poll asks Americans "Overall, how satisfied are you with the quality of education students receive in kindergarten through grade twelve in the U.S. today?," a little over half say they are dissatisfied (Gallup Poll ["Education"] 2009). (In contrast, when parents are asked "How satisfied are you with the quality of education your oldest child is receiving?," more than three-quarters report being satisfied.) The public's lukewarm confidence in schools is matched by sharper critiques from political leaders; in recent years, the term **failing schools** often found its way into the speeches of politicians from both parties. People may not agree about what it means to speak of failing schools, or about why schools are failing, or about what ought to be done to address those failures, but lots of people are willing to denounce failing schools.

Our doubts about our schools are reaffirmed by another set of news reports. Headlines such as "U.S. Trails the World in Math and Science: A Study of 12th Graders Prompts a Call for New Ways to Teach" (Bronner 1998), "Worldwide Survey Finds U.S. Students Are Not Keeping Up" (Schemo 2000), and "Math and Science Tests Find 4th and 8th Graders in U.S. Still Lag Many Peers" (Arenson 2004) have become all too familiar. Compared with students in other countries, our kids seem to be, well, stupid.

These various critiques suggest that Americans aren't as smart as they used to be, that we're experiencing what I'll call the **Stupidity Epidemic**. These are nostalgic claims, in that they imagine a better past, a time when teachers really taught and students really learned, when adults knew how to locate Louisiana on a map and could confidently match wits with fifth-graders (on **nostalgia**, see Davis 1979). Often, worries about rising stupidity are linked to warnings that the American Dream is imperiled, and there is the implication that the Stupidity Epidemic may be a specifically American problem. These are claims that describe deterioration, a society where things are getting worse, where people used to be smarter than the current, dumbest generation.

Actually, there are signs that this anxiety may not be confined to the United States. A British survey of 2,000 adults found them "historically challenged," in that they showed: "huge confusion about which characters and battles are fact and fiction. One in 10 … thought that Adolf Hitler was not a real person, and half were convinced that King Arthur existed" (Henry 2004). Canada's Dominion Institute regularly reports the results of surveys showing Canadians' inability to answer basic questions about their country's history and government (Griffiths 2007; Ipsos Reid 2009). Educational critics in England and Japan (two countries whose students usually outperform those in the U.S. in international comparisons) worry that their students don't score as well as those in still other nations (Gorard 2001; Takayama 2007). And it is worth noting that "Are You Smarter Than a 5th Grader?" has been adapted for television in nearly 50 other countries. Still, Americans seem especially concerned that we're getting dumber.

This essay explores the idea of the Stupidity Epidemic, its history, and its causes, but also evidence that can help us assess these claims. It begins with the next section, which examines the history of worries about American education's failures. It quickly becomes clear that lots of people have worried about shortcomings in Americans' knowledge, and that they have held the schools responsible. The following section turns to evidence, and asks what the data show. That is, we'll consider some ways we might measure the rising tide of ignorance, and look for evidence for the Stupidity Epidemic (spoiler alert: there isn't much evidence supporting these fears). Finally, we'll try to explain these concerns, to understand why people have misplaced fears about increasing stupidity, and consider some more constructive ways to think about the state of education.

DISCUSSION QUESTIONS

1. What sorts of evidence do critics point to when they argue that American education is failing?
2. What does the author mean by the Stupidity Epidemic?

II: Looking Backward at Fears of Failing Schools

❧

Two recent reports assessed the state of American education—*Still at Risk: What Students Don't Know, Even Now*, published by Common Core, an education advocacy group concerned with promoting the liberal arts (Hess 2008), and *Tough Choices or Tough Times*, produced by the New Commission on the Skills of the American Workforce (2007) (in turn sponsored by the National Center on Education and the Economy—another advocacy group, this one focused on education and **workforce** development). Both reports were filled with expressions of concern.

The two reports addressed different aspects of education. Common Core focused on academics; it conducted a survey that asked high school seniors fairly basic questions about history and literature, and received lots of wrong answers (e.g., only 43 percent knew the Civil War occurred between 1850 and 1900). According to *Still at Risk*:

> When it comes to familiarity with major historical events and significant literary accomplishments, America's 17-year-olds fare rather poorly…. When it comes to familiarity with the base of knowledge that enables us to engage in conversations about policy and values and so much else, our 17-year-olds are only barely literate.

> (Hess 2008: 19)

In contrast, *Tough Choices or Tough Times* took a more practical slant, and worried about young people's readiness to assume responsibilities in the workforce needed for a globalized economy. Its prognosis was stern:

> If we continue on our current course, and the number of nations outpacing us in the education race continues to grow at its current rate, the American standard of living will steadily fall relative to those nations, rich and poor, that are doing a better job.

> (New Commission on the Skills of the American Workforce 2007: 8)

Still at Risk and *Tough Choices or Tough Times* took their places on a long shelf of evaluations of the state of American education prepared by blue-ribbon commissions, professional task forces, advocacy groups, and other critics. In fact, each was a sequel to an earlier report: *Still at Risk* followed in the footsteps of 1987's *What Do Our 17-Year-Olds Know?* (Ravitch and Finn 1987); while *Tough Choices or Tough Times* succeeded a 1990 report by the original Commission on the Skills of the American Workforce (1990). Moreover, each of the new reports was timed to roughly coincide with the twenty-fifth anniversary of one of the most influential volumes on that long shelf of expert assessments.

In 1983, the National Commission on Excellence in Education (established by the U.S. Secretary of Education) issued its report, *A Nation at Risk: The Imperative for Educational Reform*. That commission produced its own grim assessment, including this often-quoted passage:

> If an unfriendly foreign power had attempted to impose on America the medio-cre educational performance that exists today, we might well have viewed it as an act of war. As it stands, we have allowed this to happen to ourselves.... We have, in effect, been committing an act of unthinking, unilateral educational disarmament.
>
> (National Commission on Excellence in Education 1983: 1)

Note some central themes in these critiques: American schools are in trouble; they may well be getting worse; and their decline stands in contrast to the improving educational systems elsewhere in the world. Other countries are raising smarties, while we're raising dummies, and if we don't watch out, they're going to eat our lunch.

Interestingly, the faces of these international rivals had changed. In 2007, *Tough Choices or Tough Times* specifically mentioned educational improvements in China and India. If the huge populations of those two giant countries attained higher levels of educational achievement, how could America hope to compete? But in 1983, when *A Nation at Risk* appeared, attention was focused on Japan, which seemed poised to become the world's dominant economic superpower (Nichols 1995). Politicians and commentators warned that Japan's yen was growing stronger against the dollar, American manufacturers were being outperformed by their Japanese counterparts, and Japanese schoolchildren were learning more than kids in U.S. schools.

Of course, *A Nation at Risk* was hardly the first such warning. The 1970s saw the appearance of worried books with titles such as *Crisis in the Classroom* and *The Literacy Hoax*. The former declared: "Our educating institutions ... all fall short of what they could be, of what they *must* be if we are to find meaning and purpose in our lives, in our society, and in our world" (Silberman 1970: 29—emphasis in original), while the latter warned: "Since the mid-1960s, academic performance and standards have shown a sharp and widespread decline" (Copperman 1978: 15).

And, if we go back a bit farther, to the late 1950s, 25 years before *A Nation at Risk*, we find an even louder clamor about the failings of American schools. The Soviet

Union's Sputnik, the first artificial satellite, launched in 1957, inspired a prolonged round of national breastbeating about the failure of American schools to keep pace with Russian science and math education. A few months after Sputnik's launch, *Life* magazine published a cover story ("Crisis in Education") with photographs contrasting the lives of two high school juniors: Alexi (from Moscow) was shown doing science experiments; while Stephen (from Chicago) was seen clustered with friends, who were trying to choose selections on a jukebox (*Life* 1958). No wonder the Russians were ahead in the space race.

Even pre-Sputnik, a host of 1950s critics warned that U.S. schools were failing. Rudolf Flesch's (1955) bestseller, *Why Johnny Can't Read*, blamed phonics for the schools' deterioration. *U.S. News and World Report* (1956) published an interview with an education professor under the title "We Are Less Educated than 50 Years Ago." Former admiral Hyman G. Rickover became a vocal educational critic, writing several books, culminating in *American Education: A National Failure* (1963). These critics made claims remarkably similar to those that would appear 25 years later (in *A Nation at Risk*) and again 50 years later (in *Still at Risk* and *Tough Choices or Tough Times*): American students aren't learning enough; in particular, they aren't being as well prepared as their counterparts elsewhere in the world (although the nations identified as having superior educational systems kept changing—from the Soviet Union in 1958, to Japan in 1983, to China and India in 2008).

The mid-century critics implied, even declared that schools used to do a better job ("We Are Less Educated than 50 Years Ago"). But if we travel back to that imagined Golden Age at the beginning of the 20th century, we find people making parallel critiques. A 1900 magazine article ("The Menace of Present Educational Methods") offered its own nostalgic recollections on a better past:

> There was a time when a teacher did not hesitate to demand personal, unaided effort and research on the part of her pupils, but now the attitude is: "Will you please to listen to what I am about to tell you and I will make it as interesting as possible?" The mental nourishment we spoon-feed our children is not only minced but peptonized so that their brains digest it without effort and without benefit and the result is the anæmic intelligence of the average American school-child.
>
> (D'Aimeé 1900: 262–63)

An English critic from the same period also used nutrition as a metaphor for education:

> The besetting sin of some modern methods of education is that they stimulate interest without laying a correspondent stress on intellectual discipline. As it were, they feed the children on sweeties and plumcake, in a strenuous revolt against an

austere tradition of too much oatmeal porridge. The American passion for candy and ice cream finds its counterpart in the schoolroom.

(Sadler 1903: 231)

Observers of the time made unfavorable comparisons between what American students learned, and the knowledge their foreign counterparts were acquiring—although their comparisons were with education in Great Britain and other Western European countries.

And yet, traveling still further back in time, in search of what early 20th century critics recalled as the more rigorous education students used to receive, we encounter other, even earlier critiques, such as *The Daily Public School in the United States*, a book published in 1866, which warned: "… the work of preparing the great body of the school children of the country for the duties and responsibilities of life, is very imperfectly done"; and "… education in our country, at the present time, is neither in character nor extent what our free political institutions demand to ensure their continuance" (Packard 1969 [1866]: 3, 13). It is not possible to go back much further in time; the first state systems for universal education were only established in the previous generation. But the reformers promoting those systems argued that they were needed precisely because local schools often failed to provide a solid education; one historian notes: "… by the 1840s, reports of the ignorance of **common-school** teachers were widespread" (Kaestle 1983: 21).

In other words, for more than a century and a half—or about as long as Americans have been requiring children to attend schools—people have been warning that those schools are not nearly good enough (Cremin 1990: 5). Parallel critiques existed regarding college students: "Throughout the 150-year history of composition instruction in American higher education, crises in students' literacy have been declared with regularity" (Stanley 2010: 1). These critiques often have been infused with nostalgia; back in the day, they've claimed, teachers had high expectations, and their students learned more than today's kids do. The critics also have insisted that other countries—initially in Europe, more recently in Asia—hold their students to much higher educational standards so that, the critics warn, the United States will soon find itself unable to compete against rival nations with better-educated populations.

No wonder Americans are concerned about a Stupidity Epidemic. For well over a century, they have been told that they ought to worry about their schools: that (1) American schools could be doing a better job; that (2) they are doing a worse job than they used to do; and that (3) other countries' schools are doing a far better job of educating their young. Now logically the first complaint—that schools could do a better job—is necessarily true and will always be true. No student can possibly learn everything; no matter how terrific the schools are, it is always going to be possible to argue that, if only the teachers and students worked harder, more learning could take place. Precisely because this claim is necessarily true, it is not especially helpful to analyze it.

However, the second criticism—that schools are actually doing worse than in the past—is not necessarily true. This is the central concern when people worry about rising stupidity—that education isn't as good as it used to be, that we are raising the dumbest generation, and that their knowledge deficit will eventually damage our entire society. These propositions may—or may not—be true, but we ought to be able to test them, to search for evidence that can tell us whether there is a Stupidity Epidemic. (In the process, we will also consider some evidence regarding the third criticism—that other nations have superior schools.)

DISCUSSION QUESTIONS

1. When did Americans begin to worry that their schools, teachers, and students ought to perform better?
2. How do images of education in other countries shape Americans' attitudes toward education? What about images of education in the past?

III: Is There Evidence That Stupidity is Increasing?

❦

Determining whether schools—or students—are doing less well than in the past demands that we compare education in at least two time periods (that is, we need to show that *Back Then* students learned X much, but *Today* they learn less than X). Such comparisons across time are routine. We can see this line of reasoning every time we hear someone say, "Back when I was in school, my teachers insisted we study, but today's teachers don't have the same high standards." This is the sort of anecdotal evidence behind those widely circulated lists contrasting the top school discipline problems in the 1940s (talking, chewing gum) with those of today (drug abuse, pregnancy). The lists' originator acknowledged: "They weren't done from a scientific survey. How did I know what the offenses in the schools were in 1940? I was there. How do I know what they are now? I read the newspapers" (O'Neill 1994: 48).

The problem is that, regardless of how sincere the speaker may be, those memories aren't especially reliable—let alone compelling—evidence. What may have seemed highly demanding to the speaker as a child might not seem so difficult to adult observers. Nor is it safe to generalize from the speaker's experiences: maybe the speaker attended especially demanding schools, or had teachers with especially high expectations, or—you get the idea.

If we want to take seriously the question of whether stupidity is on the rise, we need to be sure that we're comparing apples with apples, that is, that we're measuring the same thing in the same way at more than one time (Best 2001a). For instance, suppose that, 50 years ago someone had given every 10-year-old in America a set of math problems and recorded the scores, and that today we give the same set of problems to all of our 10-year-olds; comparing the two sets of scores would allow us to say, with reasonable confidence, that today's 10-year-olds are doing better, about the same, or worse at math than their counterparts 50 years ago. Now you might think that there would be lots of data of this sort available. When I was a student—alas, it has been more than 50 years since I was 10—we took lots of **standardized tests**. Why can't we compare the scores from back in the day with how today's kids do?

It turns out that there isn't a lot of this data available (Bracey 2006). Why not? Well, first of all, educators keep monkeying with the tests, so that differences in the sorts of questions asked make it tough to compare test scores from different years: maybe today's questions are harder—or easier—than they used to be; maybe today's tests ask questions about different topics; and so forth. Second, the population of students tested may have changed. My school may have administered a test to all 10-year-olds 50 years ago, but that test would have been given to only some—not all—kids my age. Even if every 10-year-old in my school took the test (and we can still locate the data), the results from my suburban Minnesota school wouldn't be a fair measure of how the entire nation's 10-year-olds would have done. There were tens of thousands of public school districts back then, plus private and parochial schools; only some administered any given test. It is often difficult to know how comparable the population that was tested in the past is to the students we can measure today.

All of this means that we need to be careful when we try to measure educational changes over time; it is not the simple, straightforward problem it might seem. When we do find data from different years, we need to assess just how comparable the figures are—do they measure the same sorts of people in about the same way? The task is made even more challenging because society itself is continually changing, and the way we think about education also has changed—we expect schools to perform differently.

With these warnings in mind, this section turns to four different measures of societal "stupidity": the overall level of education in the population; students' performance on tests of knowledge; the public's command of basic knowledge; and IQ scores. In all four cases, it is possible to find reasonably comparable data across a number of years, data that speak to the question of whether stupidity is increasing. If there is a Stupidity Epidemic—if we're in fact getting dumber—then we might expect to find that: (1) the level of schooling has fallen; (2) test scores have dropped; (3) surveys show that ordinary people's knowledge has declined; or (4) IQ scores have gotten lower. And, in fact, these four sets of data do tell a consistent story—but not one that supports claims about a Stupidity Epidemic. Let's look at each in turn.

Overall Level of Education

Perhaps the most basic question we might ask about a nation's educational system is about its citizens' overall level of education. What proportion of the population completes different amounts of schooling (i.e., What percentage of young people graduates from high school? From college?).

These are questions that state and federal officials have considered important, and governments have been trying to keep track of **educational attainment** in their jurisdictions for a long time. The data tell what is, overall, an unambiguous story: over time, an increasing proportion of young Americans has received more education. Consider Figure 3.1, which shows the growth in the percentage of young people graduating from high school. As late as 1910, less than one youth in ten finished high school. Most states required only that children finish what was then called "common school" (grades 1–8); thus, three of my four grandparents (all born around 1889 and raised in the rural Midwest) left school after completing eighth grade. However, the high school graduation rate soared during most of the 20th century, until it reached about 70 percent in 1960, when it began to plateau.

As Figure 3.1 shows, the graduation rate actually peaked around 1970 when it hit almost 77 percent, but has fallen back to around 70–75 percent. Is that decline proof that there is a Stupidity Epidemic? Not exactly. The figure does not include those people who leave high school, but then go on to complete **General Educational Development (GED)** or other high school equivalency credentials (Goldin 2006: Table Bc258–64; Chaplin 2002). GED programs have grown in recent decades, and the percentage of young people aged 16–24 who have not completed high school, either through graduation or a GED program, has fallen. In 1960, 27.2 percent of 16–24-year-olds had failed to complete the equivalent of a high school education; in 2008, the comparable percentage was only 8.0 percent (Goldin 2006: Table Bc480–91; National Center for Education Statistics [hereafter NCES] 2010a: Table 109). In other words,

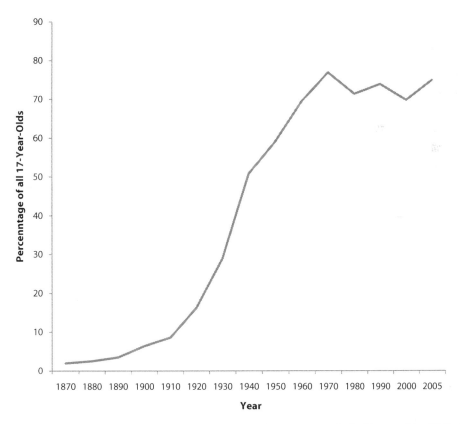

Figure 3.1 Public and private high school graduates as a percentage of all 17-year-olds, 1870–2005. *Sources:* Goldin (2006: Table Bc258–64); NCES (2005: Table 102).

Table 3.1 Percentages of High School Graduates Having Taken Selected Math and Science Courses, 1982 and 2005

Course	1982	2005
Calculus	5	14
AP Calculus	2	9
Biology	77	92
AP/Honors Biology	10	16
Chemistry	32	66
AP/Honors Chemistry	3	8
Physics	15	33
AP/Honors Physics	1	5

Source: NCES (2010a: Table 151).

at the beginning of the 20th century, less than 10 percent of young people finished high school; a century later, those with a diploma or equivalent certification exceeded 90 percent.

Not only are more students completing high school, high school graduates are taking tougher courses. Table 3.1 makes this clear. Between 1982 and 2005, all of the toughest high school math and science courses (including especially challenging **Advanced Placement [AP]** courses) enrolled increasing percentages of students.

It is important to recognize that there have been—and remain—important ethnic differences in educational attainment.[1] In 1850, 56 percent of white children (aged 5–19) were enrolled in school, in contrast to less than 2 percent of nonwhites. That gulf shrunk to a gap by 1940 (enrollment for whites was 76 percent, for nonwhites it was 68 percent), and more or less closed during the 1960s (Goldin 2006: Table Bc438–46). However, when we turn from the proportion of young people enrolled in school, to measures of school completion, racial differences remain apparent. In 2008, only 4.8 percent of whites aged 16–24 lacked either a high school diploma or a GED certificate, but the comparable percentage for blacks was 9.9 percent, and for Hispanics it was 18.3 percent (NCES 2010a: Table 108). Over time, educational attainment

---

1 At several points in this section, I will present data on ethnic differences in educational attainment, test scores, and so on. Most sociologists would argue that these differences largely reflect social class. African Americans and Hispanics have histories of discrimination and, on average, they occupy less advantaged class positions than whites, which is to say they have less education, lower incomes, less wealth, poorer health, shorter life expectancies, and other products of relatively lower class positions. These disadvantages make it harder for children to do well in school. (Lareau [2003] explains how class differences shape the upbringing children receive.) The data reveal that the more egalitarian social policies of recent decades have resulted in shrinking gaps in educational accomplishments between whites and blacks and Hispanics.

for all ethnic groups has increased; however, although the gaps between whites and nonwhites have diminished, they have not vanished.

Essentially the same story can be told for higher education: college graduates were rare at the beginning of the 20th century (see Figure 3.2); but most young people today continue their education beyond high school. For instance, an analysis of people

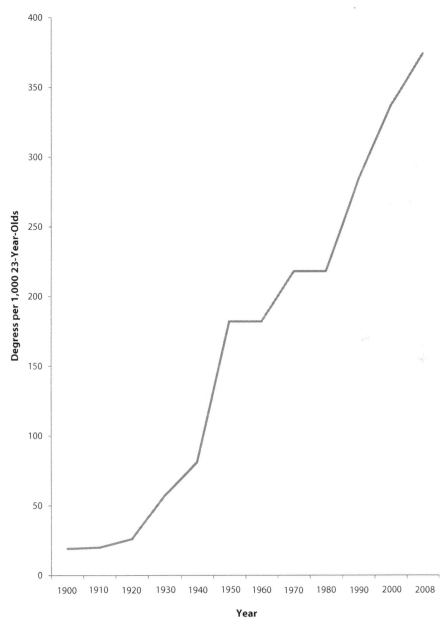

Figure 3.2 Bachelor's degrees conferred by institutions of higher education, per 1,000 persons 23 years old, 1900–2008.
Sources: Goldin (2006: Table Bc568–87); NCES (2010a: Table 268).

who were high school sophomores in 1990 found that by 2000 (10 years later), only 8.8 percent had not completed high school, while another 17.8 percent had stopped their education when they completed the equivalent of high school; that means that the rest—nearly three-quarters of the young people in that cohort—had received some sort of post-secondary education (including trade schools and community colleges) (NCES 2010a: Table 326). Most high school graduates start college, and more than a quarter of young people earn bachelor's degrees. And the same trend is found for advanced degrees. In 1900, there were only about 14 doctorates awarded per 1,000 bachelor's degrees (and remember—this was when only a tiny percentage of young people received bachelor's degrees). In 2008, when bachelor's degrees were far more plentiful, there were nearly 41 doctorates awarded per 1,000 bachelor's degrees (Goldin 2006: Table Bc568–87; NCES 2010a: Table 268).

Again, blacks and Hispanics complete both college and graduate programs at lower rates than whites, but the gaps are shrinking. Between 1977 and 2008, the number of whites earning bachelor's degrees rose 39 percent, but the increases for blacks and Hispanics were 260 percent and 657 percent, respectively. Similarly, the number of whites receiving doctor's degrees increased 37 percent, compared with 312 percent for blacks and 437 percent for Hispanics (NCES 2010a: Tables 285, 291).

Overall, the patterns are clear and consistent. The proportions of Americans completing all levels of education—high school, college, and graduate school—have increased markedly. These increases can be found in all three major ethnic groups and, while whites still attain more education than nonwhites, white–nonwhite gaps continue to close.

We might be forgiven for thinking this is a positive picture. Moreover, it isn't exactly a secret: pretty much everyone understands that more people are completing high school and college than in generations past. And yet people who are well aware of these patterns insist that there is a crisis in education—a Stupidity Epidemic. How do they manage to reconcile the familiar facts about increasing educational attainment with their fears that we are getting dumber?

The critics are able to discount statistics about educational attainment in three ways. The first is to argue that the bar has to be set higher. At the beginning of the 20th century, when both my grandfathers entered the workforce after completing eighth grade, they had fulfilled society's official expectations. Most states required that young people complete a common-school education; having learned the Three R's (reading, 'riting, and 'rithmetic), students would have had the basic intellectual training they would need to be farmers (in my grandfathers' cases) or most other sorts of workers. But, of course, educational expectations continued to rise. States began requiring that students stay in school through age 16 (in the ordinary course of things, this would be around eleventh grade), and there was a new expectation that young people should graduate from high school. By the time I was a child in the 1950s, people were talking about high school dropouts (young people who quit school before graduation) as a social problem. (This trend toward higher expectations continues; in his first State of the Union address, President Obama asked "every American to commit to at least one year or more of higher education or career training" [Levy 2009: 19].) The bar for educational achievement has been—and continues to be—raised. These elevated expectations mean that even when societal levels of education rise—and the data clearly demonstrate that this has happened—it is possible for critics to worry that Americans aren't receiving as much education as they ought to have. In their view, it doesn't matter that Americans have more education than ever before—they still don't have as much as they need.

A second critique challenges the statistics used to measure educational attainment; here, critics argue that the sorts of numbers I presented earlier paint an unrealistically rosy picture. For instance, some critics emphasize problems with statistics about dropouts. Consider, for instance, one recent front-page *New York Times* headline: "States' Inflated Data Obscure Epidemic of School Dropouts" (Dillon 2008: A1). The story's revelation that some states keep multiple sets of dropout statistics certainly sounds problematic, but it reflects an obvious fact: some students drop out before they even reach ninth grade, some during ninth grade, and so on. If you calculate dropout percentages only among those students who stayed in school to start their senior year of high school (that is, if you only count as dropouts those who leave school *during* twelfth grade), you will find that a fairly high percentage will actually graduate at the end of the year (and the dropout rate among seniors will be pretty low), so that highlighting those statistics makes your schools look good. But if you calculate the percentage of eighth-graders who go on to graduate, your dropout numbers will include those students who dropped out in eighth grade, in ninth grade, and so on—inevitably the graduation percentage will be lower, the dropout rate will seem higher, and the statistics will convey a less favorable impression of your schools. The *Times* story noted that states were often reporting more favorable figures, particularly to the federal government. The actual graduation rate—when the education of all young people is taken into account—turns out to be about 70 percent.

But this is not quite the news flash critics imply. As I noted when Figure 3.1 was introduced, the proportion of young people who graduate from high school has leveled out, and in fact is somewhat lower than it was at its peak (around 1970); in recent decades, 70–75 percent of young people have graduated from high school—down from 77 percent in 1969 (the year that percentage topped out). Critics argue that the decline in the percentage of high school graduates is a sign that things are getting worse, that fears about a Stupidity Epidemic are well founded, and they suggest that this should be considered a "national scandal." But, as we also noted, high school graduation statistics ignore those people—more than half a million each year—who complete GED programs. If we add people who earn GED certificates to those with high school diplomas, around 85 percent of the population has completed the equivalent of a high school education. But, the critics warn, a GED "is hardly equivalent to a high school diploma," as evidenced by the fact that GED recipients earn lower incomes than those who receive diplomas (Chaplin 2002: 26, 27).

Here it may help to consider the range of folks who choose to take GED exams. Probably the largest group consists of those who weren't doing well in school, dropped out, discovered that it was tough to find work without a diploma, and decided to earn a GED certificate. Those students probably had, on average, weaker academic skills than their counterparts who stayed in school and, if we assume that future income correlates with how well one does in school, it is not that surprising that these former dropouts might have lower earnings as adults. But there are other reasons individuals acquire GEDs: some students—even quite bright students—find high school boring, and use the GED as a way to escape a year or two of an experience they disdain; others' education may be derailed by a crisis (such as a teen pregnancy), and they use the GED to get back on track; or immigrants may use the GED as a means of demonstrating mastery of basic academic skills. Some of these people continue their educations well beyond the GED.

American culture celebrates **perfectibility**; we speak of social *problems*—and we think of problems as having *solutions* (Best 2001b, 2006). If we measure schools' success by whether *every* student graduates from high school (or, for that matter, completes an additional year of schooling beyond high school), we will inevitably be disappointed. On the other hand, if we treat GED certificates as fully as valuable as a high school diploma, the picture seems much brighter. In all likelihood, the truth falls somewhere between those extremes. In some cases, the GED may be a sign of weaker academic skills than a high school diploma, as the critics suggest. In 1970, roughly 77 percent of young people graduated from high school, and another 8 percent completed GEDs—85 percent total. In 2000, there were about 69 percent receiving diplomas, and another 19 percent earning GEDs—88 percent. People can disagree about the meaning of these trends (are more people getting more education [surely a good thing], or are fewer people taking the more rigorous diploma route [perhaps a bad thing]?), but it is hard to argue that they offer unambiguous evidence for a Stupidity Epidemic.

A third criticism of measures of overall level of education is that, even if the statistics are accurate, they are meaningless, because schools have debased their standards. In this view, a diploma from a high school or a college used to mean more, because students had to learn more to qualify for graduation. Back in the old days, we are told, students had to master a demanding curriculum, whereas today's kids don't have to learn all that much. Finding data to assess this critique leads us to our second set of measures.

Test Scores

Perhaps the most straightforward way to determine whether there is a Stupidity Epidemic is to compare what people know today with what people knew in the past. Such discussions usually begin with standardized test scores. It is not uncommon to hear folks bemoaning "declining test scores" as evidence that we're getting dumber; lots of people seem to assume that those scores have been getting worse, but what do the data show? (Again, remember that we're looking for apples-to-apples comparisons—similar tests, given to similar populations across time.)

Here, it will be useful to begin with **NAEP** (the **National Assessment of Educational Progress**), what the U.S. Department of Education likes to call the "nation's report card." The Department began administering NEAP in the early 1970s; it makes a determined effort to administer reading and math tests to a nationally representative sample of students at ages 9, 13, and 17 (basically grades 4, 8, and 12). The tests are designed to be as comparable as possible. This is about the best available apples-to-apples data we have that allow us to make relatively long-term comparisons.

What do the NAEP data show? Below are the summaries for the period from the beginning of testing through 2008:

> In reading, average scores … were 12 points higher than in 1971 for 9-year-olds and 4 points higher for 13-year-olds. The average reading score for 17-year-olds was not significantly different from that in 1971.
>
> In mathematics, average scores … were 24 points higher than in 1973 for 9-year-olds and 15 points higher for 13-year-olds. The average mathematics score for 17-year-olds was not significantly different from that in 1973.

(NCES 2009: 2)

In short, both series of tests show improvements for fourth- and eighth-graders, but no real change for high school seniors. Now it is of course easy to wish that the scores had risen by even larger margins, and to wish that the 17-year-olds' scores had also improved, but notice that the bottom line in the NAEP data is that scores in every group improved or stayed the same—in no group was there evidence of a Stupidity Epidemic-like decline.

But there's more. NAEP has been particularly concerned with tracking the effect of ethnicity: in both reading and math, every time the test has been given, whites have outscored blacks and Hispanics. But, in general, the gaps between whites and non-whites have been shrinking because black and Hispanic scores have been rising faster than the whites' scores. For instance, take nine-year-olds' reading scores: between 1975 and 2008, whites' scores rose 11 points, but blacks' and Hispanics' scores rose far more (23 and 24 points, respectively) (NCES 2009: 4). Essentially the same pattern: an improvement in each ethnic group's scores, but with blacks and Hispanics improving more than whites, is found for each of the three age groups on both tests (see Tables 3.2 and 3.3). Critics often shake their heads in consternation at the NAEP results: scores aren't as high as we might wish; improvements haven't been as great as we'd hoped; the gaps between ethnic groups haven't vanished. These are all legitimate concerns; of course we'd prefer news that all students were scoring off the charts. Still,

Table 3.2   Long-Term Trends in Average National Assessment of Educational Progress (NAEP) Reading Scores, by Ethnicity, 1975–2008

9-Year-Olds			
Ethnicity	1975	2008	Change
White	217	228	+11
Black	181	204	+23
Hispanic	183	207	+24
13-Year-Olds			
Ethnicity	1975	2008	Change
White	262	268	+6
Black	226	247	+21
Hispanic	232	242	+10
17-Year-Olds			
Ethnicity	1975	2008	Change
White	293	295	+2
Black	241	266	+25
Hispanic	252	269	+17

Source: NCES (2010b).

it is very difficult to examine the NAEP data and find any evidence that students are doing worse—that there is a Stupidity Epidemic.

Ah, but you might say, NAEP is just one source of data (albeit the test has been designed to offer pretty good apples-to-apples comparisons across more than 30 years). But what about **SAT (Scholastic Aptitude Test)** scores? Haven't those been declining? Well, yes—and no. Figure 3.3 summarizes the trends: average scores for all students taking the test declined markedly between 1966 and 1980: the verbal average dropped

Table 3.3   Long-Term Trends in Average National Assessment of Educational Progress (NAEP) Math Scores, by Ethnicity, 1978–2008

9-Year-Olds			
Ethnicity	1978	2008	Change
White	224	250	+26
Black	192	224	+32
Hispanic	203	234	+31
13-Year-Olds			
Ethnicity	1978	2008	Change
White	272	290	+18
Black	230	262	+32
Hispanic	238	268	+30
17-Year-Olds			
Ethnicity	1978	2008	Change
White	306	314	+8
Black	268	287	+19
Hispanic	276	293	+17

Source: NCES (2010b).

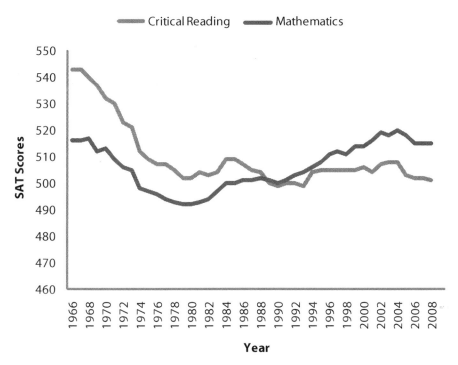

Figure 3.3   SAT scores of college-bound seniors, 1966–2006.*
*Earlier scores have been recalibrated to make them comparable across time.

from 543 to 502; the average math score fell from 516 to 492 (these numbers reflect calculations made by the College Board to make the scores comparable across time—again, so that we're comparing apples to apples). Since 1980, critical reading scores haven't changed much (the average score was 501 in 2008), while math scores rose again (to 515 in 2008).

The problem with SAT scores is that only people planning to enter college take the exam. That is, SAT scores aren't a measure of the ability of all high school seniors, but of only those intending to go to college. And as we have already noted, the percentage of high school students headed for college has risen markedly, which means that the percentage of seniors taking the SAT has increased—from less than 30 percent in 1960, to over 50 percent today (Bracey 2006: 6; College Board 2008; NCES 2010a: Table 103). As a larger share of students goes on to college (something most people would consider a good thing), those taking the SAT inevitably reflect a broader range of abilities than in the past. The College Board may be able to make its tests comparable from one year to the next, but that doesn't mean that comparable groups of students will be taking those tests.

There is an additional problem: not all college-bound students take the SAT. In general, the SAT is required by institutions in Eastern and Western states; colleges in the Midwest and South often require the **ACT** (**American College Testing**). As a result, the percentage of seniors taking the SAT varies wildly from state to state, from about 5 percent to nearly 90 percent (Powell and Steelman 1996). This results in a striking pattern: states where few students take the SAT have much higher average SAT scores than states where most students take the test. This is because SAT-taking students from, say, a Midwestern state where few take the SAT are probably intending to apply to out-of-state schools, and those ambitious youths are more likely to be better-than-average students. Because the students who choose to take the SAT vary so much, from both place to place and year to year, patterns in SAT scores are hard to interpret; certainly they do not provide unambiguous evidence that there is a Stupidity Epidemic.

But what about all of those news stories reporting that American schoolchildren perform much worse on standardized tests than their counterparts in other countries? For instance, the 2007 **Trends in International Mathematics and Science Study (TIMSS)** measured fourth- and eighth-graders. In all four rankings (that is, for both grades in both subjects), the U.S. students scored above the TIMSS average, but well below the top-scoring countries. On all four tests, the average score was scaled to 500. U.S. fourth-graders ranked 11th among 35 countries in math with an average score of 529 (Hong Kong led with a score of 607), and 8th in science with an average score of 539 (compared with Singapore's 587). Similarly, American eighth-graders had average scores of 508 in math (9th among 47 countries, behind leader Chinese Taipei with a score of 598), and 520 in science (11th behind Singapore with a score of 567) (Gonzales et al. 2008: 7, 32). There have been numerous such international comparisons in recent decades, and their results tend to resemble the 2007 TIMSS results. Typically, when critics dissect the finding of such studies, they ignore the good news (the U.S. scored above average), and emphasize the troubling findings (some other countries had higher averages).

It is rather difficult to interpret these international rankings because it is not clear that they involve apples-to-apples comparisons. The educational systems of countries differ (for instance, are all young people required to attend school?; How well does a nation's curriculum match the material covered in the test?; Are students split into academic and vocational institutions?; Are special education students enrolled in separate schools?), and these differences can affect whether the test is given only to better students, or whether a larger, more diverse proportion of the student population is being tested (for discussions of such comparability issues, see Berliner and Biddle 1995; Gorard 2001). Compared with the other G7 nations (that is, compared with the other large, industrialized nations whose economies and school systems are most like those in the United States), American students generally perform above average (Boe and Shin 2005).

In sum, there are many standardized tests—including the NAEP tests given to schoolchildren, the SAT tests given to students headed for college, or the various international comparisons such as TIMSS—and it is possible to cherry-pick findings to prove virtually any thesis, but none of these results confirm that American schools are doing especially badly, let alone getting worse.

Popular Knowledge

So far, we've focused on what's been happening in schools, and the evidence shows that, in general, young people are receiving more education and seem to do better on at least some standardized tests than in the past. But maybe the educational system can rig those data—by lowering their standards or making tests easier—so that what seems like improvement is nothing but an illusion. What about all the evidence that, out in the real world, ordinary people aren't all that smart? Remember those surveys that seem to show many people lack basic knowledge (such as being unable to find Louisiana on a U.S. map). Don't such findings suggest people are getting dumber?

There are lots of attempts to measure Americans' level of this or that sort of "literacy." For example, a 1997 poll asked Americans if they knew what the first ten amendments to the Constitution are called, and only 66 percent gave the right answer—the Bill of Rights (Roper Center for Public Opinion Research 2009: National Constitution Center survey 1997). That might seem like a fairly basic fact, one that must have been covered several times in every student's social studies and history classes. How is it possible not to know this? If only two-thirds of Americans know it, shouldn't we wonder about the nation's civic literacy? But essentially the same question has been asked in other surveys over the years: for instance, in a 1954 Gallup Poll, only 31 percent of respondents gave the right answer; in a 1991 Gallup Poll, it was 55 percent (for 1954 survey, see Delli Carpini and Keeter 1991; for 1991 Gallup Poll, see Roper Center for Public Opinion Research 2009). In other words, over time, the percentage of Americans who know that the first ten amendments are called the Bill of Rights has actually increased. The most recent percentage may seem disappointingly low, but it's higher than it used to be.

It is possible to find other basic-knowledge-of-civics questions that have been asked over the years. Table 3.4 presents results from some of these. One can read this table and feel either terribly depressed or slightly reassured. Depending on the question being asked, respondents often have tended to do somewhat better in recent years, although there are questions where the percentage of right answers has declined. It is hard to know what to make of evidence that an increasing percentage of Americans seem able to identify the political party with the most members in the U.S. Senate, even as a declining percentage can correctly identify the majority party in the House of Representatives. However, these polls do not offer unambiguous evidence that things are getting worse.

Similarly, the National Science Board (2010: Appendix Tables 7–8) examined surveys of adult Americans spanning years from 1992 to 2008 that asked various factual true–false questions (e.g., "Electrons are smaller than atoms."); the percentage of correct answers rose insignificantly, from 59 to 64 percent. Efforts to compare levels of scientific literacy in different countries reveal that the percentages of correct answers vary from question to question, and "no country consistently outperforms the others"

Table 3.4 Percentages of General Public Giving Correct Answers to Selected Questions on Civic Knowledge

Name Current U.S. Vice President	
1952	67%
1989	74%
1996	69%
2000	90%
2002	61%
2007	69%
2008	85%
Name at Least One Current U.S. Senator from Respondent's State	
1945	57%
1989	55%
1995	61%
Which Party Has Most U.S. Senators?	
1947	56%
1989	55%
1996	76%
Which Party Has Most Members in U.S. House of Representatives?	
1947	63%
1989	68%
2002	44%
2006	54%
Name Current Governor of Respondent's State	
1945	79%
1989	74%
2007	66%

Sources: 1989 and earlier: Delli Carpini and Keeter (1991: 591–93); 1995 and later: Roper Center for Public Opinion Research (2009: 1995–*Washington Post*; 1996 [Vice Pres.]–CNN/*USA Today*; 1996 [Senate]–*Washington Post*/Kaiser; 2000–Gallup; 2002 [Vice Pres.]–Pew Research; 2002 [House]–Chicago Council on Foreign Relations; 2006–Pew/AP/AOL; 2007–[both]–Pew Research; 2008–*Time*).

(National Science Board 2010: 7–23). While these findings are nothing to cheer about, they hardly confirm the existence of a Stupidity Epidemic.

In fact, critics tend to see any improvements in people's performance as almost irrelevant to the larger pattern of appalling ignorance. Thus, a newspaper story reports: "while *scientific literacy has doubled* over the past two decades, only 20 to 25 percent of Americans are 'scientifically savvy and alert'" (Dean 2005: 3—emphasis added). Further, critics argue, modest improvements can be discounted because the overall level of education has increased; if larger shares of the population are graduating from high school or completing college, then shouldn't we expect more substantial improvements in the proportions answering the survey questions correctly (Delli Carpini and Keeter 1991)? Of course, we might wish that more people performed better on these polls. Still, these measures do not prove that there is an epidemic of stupidity; if anything, they hint at modest gains in popular knowledge.

We can find people worrying about civic literacy, scientific literacy, even sexual literacy. But what about good, old-fashioned, ability-to-read-and-write literacy? In the 1870 census, people were considered illiterate if they could not read or write in any language, and 20 percent of the population was classified as illiterate. The percentage of people who are—by this standard—illiterate has declined sharply; an estimate for 1979 was that only 0.6 percent of Americans could not read or write (Goldin 2006: Table Bc793–97). Literacy, then, seems to have become effectively universal.

And yet, in recent decades, there have been numerous claims that illiteracy is a major problem in the U.S., one that affects tens of millions of people. In 1985, the educational critic Jonathan Kozol's book, *Illiterate America*, attracted widespread attention when it charged that 60 million adults had "from marginal [reading] ability to none at all" (Kozol 1985: 11). That same year, Rudolf Flesch (still promoting phonics 30 years after publishing *Why Johnny Can't Read*) declared: "The National Institute of Education … says that 27 million adults are wholly illiterate and 45 million more are near-illiterate"; only one year later, the *New York Times* reported "Prof. Jeanne Chall of Harvard University recently estimated that as many as 75 million to 85 million of 180 million adult Americans are unable to read or write" (Flesch 1985: A19; Gruson 1986: C11). Headlines for other *Times* stories offered a variety of large, albeit very different estimates of the problem's size: "Study Says 5% of Young Adults Are Illiterate" (*New York Times* 1986: A28); "13% of U.S. Adults Are Illiterate in English, a Federal Study Finds" (Werner 1986: A1); "Study Says Half of Adults in U.S. Lack Reading and Math Abilities" (Celis 1993: A1). How is it possible that apparently authoritative estimates for the extent of illiteracy among adults can range from less than 1 percent to as much as 50 percent?

The answer lies in multiple definitions of illiteracy. Once considered the ability to read at all, literacy has been redefined as the ability to read *well enough*. Almost all of the people described as "wholly illiterate" are able to read basic texts; their illiteracy refers to the limited nature of their reading skills. Proponents of this view speak of **functional literacy**, which is variously defined as an ability to read at a third-grade, or even a sixth-grade level; or in terms of being able to decipher a bus schedule or compose a letter complaining about a billing error. Inevitably, the higher the bar is set for being considered functionally literate, the smaller the share of the population that meets the standard, and the larger proportion of people labeled illiterate.

Consider the **National Assessment of Adult Literacy**, a 2003 study conducted by the U.S. Department of Education, designed to be comparable to an earlier 1992 study (Kutner et al. 2007). This research examined three different forms of literacy: prose literacy (the ability to comprehend and use information written in continuous texts, such as a news story or a set of instructions), document literacy (the ability to comprehend other sorts of written materials, such as forms, labels, and schedules), and quantitative literacy (the ability to comprehend and work with numbers embedded in printed materials). Each form of literacy was divided into four levels: Below Basic, Basic, Intermediate, and Proficient. For instance, individuals classified as Below Basic in prose literacy might be completely unable to read and write, but they also might be able to "identify what it is permissible to drink before a medical test, based on a short set of instructions," or "find information in a short, simple prose passage" (Kutner et al. 2007: 5). In comparison, individuals scored as having Basic prose literacy had somewhat more sophisticated skills, such as being able to "find information in a pamphlet for prospective jurors that explains how citizens were selected for the jury pool," and so on. In other words, these studies defined literacy as more than just a simple ability to read.

The 2003 National Assessment of Adult Literacy found relatively no change in overall prose and document literacy from 1992, and a modest improvement in quantitative literacy. In 2003, for instance, the classification for levels of prose literacy was: Below Basic—14 percent; Basic—29 percent; Intermediate—44 percent; and Proficient—13 percent; among those aged 16–24, 11 percent were classified as Below Basic, compared with 23 percent of those aged 65 and older—hardly evidence that successive generations were becoming less literate (Kutner et al. 2007: 12–13, 28). As we might expect, based on what we know about levels of educational attainment and test scores, whites had generally higher levels of literacy than African Americans and Hispanics, those who had completed more schooling displayed higher levels of literacy, and so on.

Again, these results do not support the idea of a Stupidity Epidemic. There is no evidence that actual levels of literacy have declined, although it is clear that our standards for judging literacy have risen. Someone may have limited skills, such as being able to understand written instructions regarding what to eat and drink before a medical test, yet still be considered to be of inadequate—Below Basic—literacy. Of course, the critics do have a point. Modern society increasingly expects people to be able to display all sorts of reading and writing skills (consider the growing importance of computer literacy—the ability to navigate around the Internet, to use a word processor, and so on). Ideally, all citizens would be able to read and comprehend even the most complicated, nearly impenetrable prose, and clearly lots of people fall well short of that level of competency, and those with fewer skills face serious consequences—fewer job opportunities, lower incomes, and so on. But wishing that more people were more literate does not allow us to conclude that there is a Stupidity Epidemic making things worse.

Well, most people may be able to read, but what are they reading? There is evidence that fewer people read books than in the past. Surveys by the National Endowment for the Arts (NEA) show that the percentage of adult Americans who reported that they read any book in the previous year declined from 61 percent in 1992, to 57 percent in 2002, to 54 percent in 2008 (NEA 2004: 4; NEA 2008: 7). Critics view this as a disturbing trend, given that not reading is associated with lower levels of educational achievement, and students who report reading more tend to do better in school (NEA 2007). This decline in book reading seems consistent with claims for a Stupidity Epidemic, although it probably should not be taken as proof that reading in general is declining. People are reading less on paper, and more via the internet and other electronic platforms. For instance, fewer people are reading newspapers (the percentage of Americans reading a Sunday newspaper fell from about 75 percent in 1964, to about 55 percent in 2007), but more than a third of Americans now read newspaper web sites (Newspaper Association of America 2010). Certainly some forms of reading matter have shrinking audiences, but given technological changes in what is available to be read, the evidence for a decline in reading is not clear-cut.

In some cases, critics make confident, straightforward assertions that things have actually deteriorated. One claim that has been repeated many times is that researchers have found that the vocabularies of young Americans have been shrinking, that, at the end of World War II, the average grade school student knew 25,000 words, but that the comparable figure today is only 10,000 words. Think about that for a moment, in the light of what we've already established: Americans are getting more schooling; and students test scores have risen. Is it likely, even plausible that students' vocabularies are only a fraction of what they were two generations ago? Of course not.

And, in fact, this supposed decline reflects two very different measures of vocabulary size—a failure to compare apples with apples. The larger figure comes from a 1936 study of more than 100,000 writing samples from schoolchildren (the research was reported in a book published in 1947); the compositions did contain more than 25,000 different words, although more than 11,000 of these were used by only one or two children (Rinsland 1947). In other words, there is no reason to think that the "average" child knew anything like all 25,000 words. The smaller figure comes from a 1979 study of more than 4,000 student writing samples; these contained more than 10,000 different words (of which about 5,000 appeared in only one or two students' work) (Smith and Ingersoll 1984).

There are two problems with comparing the two studies. The first, of course, is their wildly different sample sizes—100,000 vs. 4,000 pieces of writing. The bigger the sample, the greater the total number of words (6,012,359 total words in the 1936 study, compared with only 482,487 in the 1979 study), and therefore more different words can be expected to appear in the writing; we shouldn't be surprised that the vastly larger sample generated more different words. Second, neither study attempted to estimate students' average vocabulary size. Instead, the researchers were more interested in which words were used more often. There was a lot of overlap: over 3,000 of the 5,000 words appearing most often in the 1945 study were among the 5,000 most frequently used words in 1984. But times change. The authors of the latter study offer examples of words in their sample that were not used by any of the earlier study's students, including: abortion, addicted, assassinate, brutality, corruption, euthanasia, fuel-efficient, ghetto, holocaust, junkie, marijuana, molested, mugged, nuclear, over-populated, overdose, pollution, panic-stricken, power-mad, prefabricated, push-button, radiation, sixpack, slums, smog, terrorized, tranquilizers, warheads, and zillionaire (Smith and Ingersoll 1984: 24–25). These suggest that vocabularies are changing, not that they are shrinking.

In short, when we try to measure popular knowledge—what ordinary people know—it is again hard to find evidence that things are getting worse. If anything, there are signs of some improvement. At this point, we've found that schooling has increased, that test scores are up (a bit), and that popular knowledge also seems somewhat improved. But that's not all; there's a fourth measure that challenges claims about a Stupidity Epidemic.

IQ Scores

Level of education, standardized test scores, and surveys of general knowledge are all indirect measures of societal stupidity; if there is a Stupidity Epidemic—if people are getting dumber or we're raising the dumbest generation—we ought to expect these measures to decline. But isn't there a more straightforward way of assessing overall intelligence (or stupidity)? Isn't that exactly what **IQ tests** ought to tell us? If we're getting dumber, we would expect IQs to be falling.

Intelligence testing emerged in the early 20th century, at a time when many people were enamored with the ideas of **eugenics**—that social policy should encourage reproduction among the healthiest people and discourage it among the least healthy. Eugenicists argued that intelligence was inherited, and that people of low intelligence (at the time, the polite term was **feebleminded**) were disproportionately responsible for crime, drunkenness, and other social problems. Moreover, the feebleminded were thought to reproduce at higher rates than people of higher intelligence; eugenicists warned that the feebleminded threatened the future, that humanity was headed toward "race suicide." These fears became justifications for sterilizing many feebleminded people. Since the poor, immigrants, and members of ethnic minorities tended to have lower IQ scores, the "menace of the feebleminded" was associated with those disadvantaged sectors of society (Trent 1994).[2] Eugenics fell out of

---

2 There is a long-running debate about what IQ tests actually measure. Their proponents (including those early eugenicists) argue that differences in IQ scores among social classes or ethnic groups reflect real differences in natural ability (Herrnstein and Murray, 1994). Their critics (including most sociologists) counter that test scores are greatly determined by the different social circumstances in which children are raised, and that changing social conditions can raise IQs (Fischer et al. 1996).

favor after the world recoiled in horror from the policies of its most enthusiastic advocates—the Nazis.

This does not mean that eugenic arguments have vanished from our popular thinking. Consider the opening scenes of *Idiocracy*, a movie comedy released in 2006, where we see a yuppie couple—sincere, highly educated, socially concerned—who keep finding reasons to delay parenthood and eventually die without having kids, and a trailer-trash couple—dim-witted hedonists—who proliferate like mad. The bottom line: smart people have fewer kids than stupid people, with the result—the futuristic society portrayed in the movie—that society grows ever dumber. *Idiocracy* plays this idea for laughs, but the fear that the least intelligent sectors of society have higher birthrates, and that we must as a result be growing dumber, turns up in popular thought.

It is, therefore, somewhat surprising to discover that this fear is completely misplaced, that IQ scores have been steadily rising, not falling. This is the so-called **Flynn effect**, named after the New Zealand political scientist James R. Flynn, who drew it to scholars' attention (Flynn 2009). The process went largely unnoticed because psychologists who measure intelligence continually recalibrate how IQ tests are scored. This is because psychologists think of IQs as being normally distributed along the familiar bell-curve distribution; they define the average score as an IQ of 100. In other words, 100 is not some number of correct answers to IQ test questions; 100 is whatever turns out to be the average number of correct answers. Thus, the average IQ in 1950 was 100; so is the average IQ today. However, that does not mean that those two apparently equal scores represent the same number of correct answers on an IQ test. Frame the question differently: take the number of correct answers that would produce an average (100) score in 1950; if someone took the test today and gave the same answers, what score would he or she receive? Would you believe, 82? IQs have increased about 18 points in the last 60 years—about 3 points per decade. The long-term effect is shocking:

> Imagine this scenario: a person who tests in the top 10 percent of the United States in 1920 time-travels eighty years into the future and takes the [IQ] test again. Thanks to the Flynn Effect, he would be in the bottom third for IQ scores today. Yesterday's brainiac is today's simpleton.
>
> (Johnson 2005: 142–43)

The Flynn Effect is a remarkably robust finding; it has been documented in some 30 countries—many in the United States or Europe, but also in the developing world. If intelligence is what IQ tests measure, then the 20th century saw a marked increase in intelligence.

How is this possible? Were our parents' and grandparents' generations really much stupider than ours? No. IQ tests measure abstract thinking skills, and there are lots of reasons to believe that we live in a world that places a much higher value on those forms of thinking. Our schools place more emphasis on—and do a better job of teaching—some of those skills, which in turn means that this generation performs better on those sections of IQ tests. And it's not just schools. Popular culture has become more complex; we have to think harder to play today's more complicated video games, or follow the more complex plots on current television shows. We live in a world that rewards abstract thinking and, as a consequence, more people are getting better at it, and performance on IQ tests is improving.

Flynn offers this example:

> Assume we hear a recent high school graduate chatting with his grandfather (who also finished high school) … . There is no reason to believe either would have to make allowance for the obtuseness of the other … . There is no reason to believe either would strike us as inferior to the other in terms of vocabulary or fund of general information. [However] we would be likely to notice some differences. The grandson would be … more adept at dealing with novel problems posed verbally or visually or abstractly. Sometimes, the grandfather's "handicap" would affect conversation, particularly because he would not think that such problems were very important. The grandfather might be more rule-governed and would probably count that as a virtue.
>
> (Flynn 2009: 22–23)

Some critics warn that the Flynn Effect may soon taper off, that IQ scores cannot keep continuing to rise, at least not in the developed world. The Flynn Effect says more about how intelligence is measured, than it does about some remarkable evolution in human powers. Nonetheless, changes in IQ scores—like the other measures we used to look for evidence of a Stupidity Epidemic—provide no support for claims that we're getting dumber. In fact, depending on how you define intelligence, we seem to be getting smarter.

Confronting the Evidence

So, what have we discovered? When we look for hard evidence—for apples-to-apples comparisons across time—it is hard to find much support for claims that Americans are getting dumber. Americans receive more education than in the past. Their standardized test scores show some improvement. There is no unambiguous evidence that popular knowledge has declined, and there are some indications it may have increased a bit. And IQ scores have been rising. Now, a critic might easily argue that all of these changes show only modest, gradual progress, that society would be better off if more people knew more, that troubling class and ethnic gaps remain. Things aren't prefect, we can agree. Still, fears about a Stupidity Epidemic—calling today's youth the dumbest generation and so on—seem misplaced. Things aren't getting worse fast; in fact, they seem to be getting better (albeit slowly).

In a sense, that should be no surprise. Many of us can see evidence of rising levels of education in our own families: lots of us have more education than our parents; our parents received more education than our grandparents; and so on. I went to a pretty good suburban high school, and I took the toughest math courses it offered; in my senior year, our studies took us through trigonometry. Both my sons went to schools not that different from mine, but both had at least a year of calculus in high school. (That's not to say that there weren't some bad teachers and disappointing classes in my sons' schooling—I have stories like that, too.) But their high school math courses were harder than mine. My family's history—and I suspect this is true for many other people's families—is one of people getting more, and better, schooling. Most of us know this. When we worry about the Stupidity Epidemic, we worry it's affecting other people, not ourselves.

Yet, in spite of all of the evidence—not just the sorts of statistical evidence we've reviewed in this section, but also the evidence from our own lives—that should cause us to doubt claims about a Stupidity Epidemic, those claims remain fairly common. How can we explain this? Why do people accept the idea our society is getting dumber, even when their personal experiences suggest that's not true? There are several answers to this question, which are the subject of the next section.

DISCUSSION QUESTIONS

1. The author emphasizes the need to make apples-to-apples comparisons when measuring changes in education. What does this mean? What are some ways data might fail to meet the apples-to-apples standard?

2. Summarize the long-term trends in educational attainment. What are some reasons people might conclude these are positive? Why might others find them worrisome?

3. It is not uncommon for critics to speak of falling SAT scores. What do the scores show? Discuss why it is difficult to compare SAT scores across time.

4. You read a news story about Americans' poor performance on a test of economic literacy. What questions might you ask?

5. What is the Flynn Effect, and what does it tell us about societal intelligence?

IV: Explaining the Concern

෴

A lthough there may not be much good evidence to support claims about a Stupidity Epidemic, people nonetheless manage to worry about it. Why? How can we explain this contradiction? This section examines six reasons why we continue to hear warnings about the Stupidity Epidemic.

Stupidity May Not Be Increasing, but Ignorance Is

We might begin by distinguishing between stupidity and ignorance. We have been talking about stupidity in terms of lacking basic knowledge and intellectual skills—what we might think of as fundamental resources needed to manage successfully within society. Again, the evidence does not suggest that stupidity is on the rise. Ignorance, in contrast, refers to what we don't know, and it is inevitably increasing at a rapid clip.

We live in what some sociologists call a **knowledge society**, one that is continually generating massive amounts of new information (Ungar 2003). There are millions of people whose jobs are to generate new knowledge—just think of all of the scientists in all of the disciplines. Many of them are engaged in research; that is, they create new knowledge. Ignore, for the moment, those who are producing proprietary knowledge—developing, say, new drugs for the benefit of the pharmaceutical companies that employ them—and who keep their new knowledge secret. Just consider those who make their contributions public, who share the knowledge they've generated through publishing their research results in professional journals. There are tens of thousands of those journals. It is impossible for anyone to keep up with all of them, with all of the new knowledge. Not only is it impossible to stay abreast of all scientific developments, it is not even possible for a scientist to stay abreast of his or her own scientific discipline, nor even for a specialist to follow all of the developments within his or her chosen specialty within that discipline.

This produces what some sociologists call **KIP—the knowledge–ignorance paradox**: "the growth of specialized knowledge implies a simultaneous increase in (general) ignorance" (Ungar 2008: 311). Even if all Americans devote all of their time to acquiring knowledge, so that each personally learns a lot, at the end of each day the proportion of the world's knowledge that each of them knows will have declined. They may be less stupid, but they inevitably become more ignorant.

Notice that KIP is not restricted to academic knowledge. The world is filled with increasing stocks of information. It is impossible to watch all of the movies, read all of the new romance novels, evaluate all of the available mutual funds, stay on top of all sports news, and so on. Thanks to the Internet, we are increasingly aware that we have myriad choices; in order to make wise selections, we tend to rely on the advice of critics, ratings services, and other arbiters who presumably have lots of specialized knowledge and can advise us on our options (Blank 2007).

One consequence of this diversity of choices is that it becomes less and less likely that lots of people will make the same choice. For the first 30 years Americans had televisions, most of them depended on broadcast signals; that is, they received only those channels whose signals were within range of their antennae. In practice, this meant that most Americans could watch a handful of channels—ABC, CBS, and NBC network affiliates, maybe an educational channel, and perhaps one or two independent stations. At any given time, about 90 percent of people were likely to be watching one of the three networks, so each network had about 30 percent of the viewers tuned in to its programs. Today, of course, the world seems much different. Most TVs receive cable or satellite signals, so that viewers can choose among dozens, even hundreds of channels (or they may use their televisions to play games, watch DVDs, and so on). It has become quite unlikely that 30 percent of Americans will watch even a top-rated program on network TV. Compared with a few decades ago, fewer people know what happened last night on any particular TV program, although lots of people may have seen some of the many programs shown. In other words, ignorance is increasing for all sorts of knowledge, not just for serious scientific research findings, but even for the most frivolous sorts of popular knowledge

The realization that we are constantly confronted by decisions that turn out to involve an unmanageable array of choices, as well as our increased reliance on specialized assistance to guide us, can give us the sense that the world is becoming unmanageably complex. Of course this was always true; it is probably impossible to identify a date when the total stock of human knowledge wasn't increasing faster than any individual could hope to keep pace. But in the past the full range of our ignorance was more likely to be concealed by our limited social networks; we had trouble realizing what—and how much—we didn't know. But today's wired world gives us a clearer sense of how much we don't—can't possibly—know. And, in turn, our frustration and confusion, caused by our increasing realization that other people don't know what we know, may lead us to imagine that the problem is a rising tide of stupidity.

What We Know—and Don't Know—Keeps Changing

In 1931, Yale College declared that its students would no longer be required to study Latin and Greek (*New York Times* 1931b). This marked a significant break with tradition. For centuries higher education meant being trained in the classics, reading the works of the Greek and Roman historians, poets, and philosophers in their original languages. However, in the 19th century, reformers began arguing that the ancient languages should no longer be required, that, since Aristotle's four elements and four humors no longer served as central concepts in science and medicine, it was more important to study more recent works, written in modern languages, than to master ancient tongues. Thorstein Veblen, for instance, railed against educators "consuming the learner's time and effort in acquiring knowledge which is of no use" (Veblen 1953 [1899]: 254).

Yale's decision to drop Latin and Greek was controversial. There were those who argued that something important would be lost; the *New York Times* interviewed an emeritus professor from Princeton who declared:

> I think it would be a great pity, a real disaster, if Latin and Greek should drop out of the educational program of our American universities. No other studies, with the possible exception of mathematics, have proved as valuable for the training of the mind in clear thought and accurate expression.... The best hope of restoring the English language from its present slip-shod condition lies in a revival of the study of Latin.
>
> (*New York Times* 1931a: 18)

Obviously, once the reforms took effect, those educated under the new system would now know less—that is, less Latin and Greek—than their predecessors. This is a process that is repeated every time an educational curriculum changes. When I was a high school student, we learned to use slide rules in math and science classes; however, I suspect that few of my students have even seen a slide rule, and that none of them command the slipstick skills I once had. At the end of World War II, many Ph.D. programs required that students demonstrate competence in two foreign languages; by the 1960s, doctoral programs increasingly allowed students to substitute familiarity with a computer language (such as having an ability to program in FORTRAN) or statistics as equivalent to one foreign language. Today, many doctoral programs do not have any foreign language or computer programming requirements, but they often demand that students take several courses in advanced statistics. In other words, time and again, schools have stopped teaching material that used to be considered educationally important.

The justification for changing these requirements is related to shifts in what are understood to be necessary intellectual skills. It is not that graduating from Yale or earning a Ph.D. has become necessarily easier (although this is what is implied when people worry that standards are being "watered down"). Rather, today's requirements are different than those of the past. Sure, probably lots of students used to struggle with Latin and Greek, so eliminating those requirements ended those obstacles to earning a Yale degree. But those requirements were replaced by others. Slide rules fell out of the high school curriculum, but computers were added. Probably some Ph.D. students find it harder to master French than advanced statistics, but there are doubtless others who find languages easier.

In other words, what we assume an educated person should know—what schools ought to require students to learn before they can graduate—changes. We can see the same thing in everyday life. We are surrounded by ever more complex technological devices; a generation ago, many adults struggled trying to program their **VCR**s. Today, the simplest cell phones—devices that many elementary schoolchildren master—offer a far more complicated set of options than those VCRs. Now it is also the case that much practical knowledge has been lost; far fewer people are able to do routine maintenance on their cars than in generations past, and almost no one knows how to properly harness a horse to a buggy.

It is always possible to point to knowledge that more people used to have—how to harness a horse or read Greek—and argue that people don't know as much as they used to, and that this is indicative of a general decline in knowledge. But the flip side of that claim is that people now know lots of things that no one knew in the past. The fact that what is considered socially relevant knowledge changes allows critics to point to what people no longer know as evidence that there is a Stupidity Epidemic: "As often as not, [the charge of declining academic standards] suggests that young people are learning less of what a particular commentator or group of commentators believe they ought to be learning ..." (Cremin 1990: 7). But this is a critique which counts only what has been lost, and ignores all that has been gained.

More Access to Education Increases the Range of Student Abilities

There is another effect of changes in American education. At the beginning of the 20th century, only about 2 percent of young Americans attended college. Now certainly the opportunity to receive a higher education was not evenly distributed; it was more difficult for women to go to college than it was for men, for blacks compared with whites, for youths who grew up in rural areas compared with their urban counterparts. But, even taking these social obstacles into account, we might guess that the great majority of the 2 percent who made it to college came from, say, the smartest third of the population, or at least the third who were the best students. Doubtless there were some not-so-smart sons of wealthy parents who landed in college, but it's hard to imagine that early 20th century colleges were filled with students of only average or even below-average intelligence, ability, and motivation.

As the 20th century progressed, access to college increased. The old barriers of sexism, racism, and geography may not have vanished, but they certainly became more permeable. Remember that currently most young people start college. Obviously all of those students—more than half the population—can't all come from the most able third. A more accessible system of higher education—something that most people would consider a good thing—is less elitist, not just in the sense that it is less likely to celebrate the superiority of its students, but in the sense that those students include people who probably wouldn't have been considered college material in the past.

Of course, this does not mean that today's students are unqualified. If they have in fact learned more in high school than students used to, and if the population's intelligence has been increasing via the Flynn Effect, we might reasonably suspect that a larger share of the population is in fact capable of doing college-level work. Remember, too, that in the Good Old Days, there were lots of bright, capable students whose routes to college were blocked. Still, the range of college students' abilities is also likely to have increased. A century ago, most of the students professors saw probably ranged in intelligence from the very brightest to those who were only smarter than, say, two-thirds or three-fifths of the population. Today, the very brightest students are still there, but the skills of the least able students may only be better than those of 40 percent—perhaps only a quarter or a third—of the population, which inevitably means that there will be a big range of abilities among the students. (The same thing happens when high schools reduce drop-out rates; those students who remain in school will feature a growing proportion of less-able students.)

For more than a century, critics of higher education have expressed dismay at the proportion of students who require remedial work (classes once dismissed as "bone-head English") (Stanley 2010). This is often taken to indicate that high schools aren't doing their job, that today's college students are worse prepared than their counterparts in the past—in short, that there's a Stupidity Epidemic. But this may also be an artifact of admitting a growing proportion of students to college: a student who requires remedial courses today might not have been admitted in the past. Indeed, critics sometimes point to new waves of students, such as Second World War veterans or immigrants, to explain why remedial courses are needed, even as they note the importance of educating these new sorts of students. But the need for remediation never ends. A pessimist might warn that this reflects a decaying educational system, but an optimist might argue that it is desirable to open the doors to higher education and give more people a chance to succeed. After all, some of those students taking remedial coursework will profit from the experience, and go on to graduate. Would society really be better served if they were kept out of college?

American attitudes toward education reflect a tension between a democratizing desire to give more people more education, and meritocratic assumptions that more education reflects greater abilities. If more students are staying in schools, we worry that schools must be lowering their standards, even though—as we have seen—there is evidence that schools have gotten more, not less demanding. This tension has a long history, as evidenced by our enduring fears about the Stupidity Epidemic.

We Expect a Lot from Schools

Observers who worry about the Stupidity Epidemic often point to ethnic differences in student performance. As we have seen, whites tend to stay in school longer than blacks and Hispanics; similarly, whites tend to receive higher scores on standardized tests and IQ tests. These ethnic differences are viewed as troubling. We of course live in a society where whites tend to have more advantages than blacks and Hispanics—they live longer, have higher incomes and greater wealth, and such. If we hold to the American Dream, then we need to believe that our society welcomes black and Hispanic achievement, that avenues to getting ahead are open, so that eventually no ethnic group should be disadvantaged in longevity or income.

The same ideas govern American's thinking about most sorts of inequality. On the one hand, ours is a society with a lot of inequality, and it has been growing. The gulf between our society's most advantaged and least advantaged members has increased (Frank 2007). On the other hand, public opinion polls reveal that most Americans do not view this situation as especially unfair, that they believe that people with a lot of advantages have worked hard and deserve what they have. For instance, in a 2007 poll, 62 percent of Americans disagreed with the statement: "Success in life is pretty much determined by forces outside our control" (Pew Research Center for the People and the Press 2007: 15). We believe that ours is a society that is especially open to individual advancement, that hard work pays off, so that those who strive can improve their lot. In other words, we both celebrate equality and accept a fair amount of inequality.

In part, we are able to balance these apparently contradictory ideas by viewing education as the great escalator to upward mobility and equality. Even children from quite disadvantaged backgrounds can, we like to think, acquire the education needed to get ahead in life. In America, every child is encouraged to stay in school. How are kids from disadvantaged backgrounds supposed to get ahead? By studying hard, of course. So news that black and Hispanic students don't do as well as white students is worrying because it suggests that that egalitarian American Dream won't be coming true anytime soon.

There are competing explanations for ethnic differences in education. Critics on the left tend to attribute them to structural inequalities: on average, black and Hispanic students attend schools that are less well-equipped, have more limited budgets, and are staffed with less qualified, less dedicated teachers. In this view, the educational system is structured in a way that reproduces the inequalities in society. In contrast, critics on the right are more likely to argue that ethnic differences are a product of qualities of the students. This can take the form of arguing that there are fundamental ethnic differences in intelligence that explain the weaker school performance by black and Hispanic students (Herrnstein and Murray 1994). However, it is not necessary to claim that differences in educational achievement are rooted in biology. Other conservative critics argue that there are cultural differences, that ethnic subcultures may discourage academic achievement (Ogbu 2008). For whatever reason, disproportionate shares of black and Hispanic students wind up doing relatively poorly.

In trying to explain ethnic differences in student performance, schools become an attractive scapegoat. Americans act as though they believe schools should be able to even out social inequalities by giving all young people the intellectual skills they will need to succeed. If black and Hispanic students perform less well than whites, their teachers and schools have failed—hence politicians' fondness for talking about failing schools: continued inequality can be blamed on the Stupidity Epidemic.

No doubt it is possible to improve the schools and teachers that serve disadvantaged children; after all, it is always possible to imagine ways to improve. But notice what the focus on failing schools ignores. Class, not ethnicity, has the greatest impact on student performance. Kids from poorer homes are more likely to have less educated parents, they are more likely to live with a single parent, they probably grew up with fewer books in the home, on average their neighbors have less education than average (because those who gain more education and acquire higher-paying jobs are likely to move out of poorer neighborhoods), and so on. In other words, these children are likely to grow up in environments that downplay—or at least don't do enough to promote—the importance of education, and that offer less support for students who are trying to do well in school. Many critics, including many sociologists, would argue that, instead of concentrating solely on the schools' shortcoming, reformers who are worried about the poor academic performance of nonwhites should focus on doing more to diminish the effects of class inequality (Ravitch 2010). Blaming the Stupidity Epidemic is a convenient way to avoid confronting the larger problem of inequality in America.

Scaring People Works

Throughout this essay, I have referred to the "critics" or "reformers" who warn of the Stupidity Epidemic. Who are these people, and what do they want?

Sociologists who study social problems challenge the commonsensical view that social problems are readily visible conditions in society (Best 2008). Rather, sociologists argue someone must bring these problems to our attention, get us to understand that this particular condition is troubling, and that we ought to do something to eliminate it, or at least reduce its harmful effects. This process is termed the **social construction** of social problems. Educational critics and reformers, then, are those who draw attention to—who socially construct—problems with schools and teachers. The history of education features many examples of such claims: the early 19th century calls for states to make public education universally available to all children; later reforms requiring that children stay in school until they completed a particular grade or reached some specified age; the campaign to end racially segregating schooling; and so on.

People who seek to construct educational problems find themselves in a competition to gain the attention of the press (which can relay their message to many people), members of the public (who can demand changes from their leaders), and the policy makers (who have the power to make those changes). But educational reformers are hardly the only people clamoring to be noticed. At any given moment, there are many different advocates competing to draw attention to different sorts of social problems—crime problems, medical problems, family problems, and so on (Best 2008; Hilgartner and Bosk 1988). No one can listen to all of these competing voices. Imagine a team of television journalists working to prepare a news program; they find themselves sorting through countless possible stories, trying to choose the few that they will cover (and deciding which of those stories deserves to go first—to be treated as the most important). Similar choices occur when lawmakers decide which bills deserve priority, or which programs most need to be funded. It is not enough that advocates speak up about some social problem; they must make their claims compelling enough that people will be sure to listen.

One of the best ways for them to do this is to make their claims alarming. Presenting a social problem as a threat is an effective way to grab people's attention, to make them concerned about the advocates' issue. Scaring people often works: it makes them worried. Of course, many advocates promoting all sorts of problems know this, which is why we are bombarded by claims about threatening conditions. This competition among claims encourages a sort of escalation, as advocates struggle to make their concerns seem more compelling than their rivals', they find themselves describing their problems in ever more alarming terms.

Concern about the Stupidity Epidemic fits this pattern. We have already seen that data regarding education tell a story of long-term progress—more students getting more education, and so on. That story is unlikely to arouse people's concern, to convince them that improving education is an urgent matter. If education's advocates emphasize talk about progress, their concerns may seem less compelling than rival, scarier claims about other issues, and the press, the public, and policy makers are likely to focus their attention on what seem to be the more pressing concerns. It is far more effective to portray education as a serious problem, to talk about failing schools, and describe today's students as the dumbest generation (Hampel 1986). Almost any issue can be constructed in scary terms. For instance, efforts to expand programs for gifted children (that is, for those student who already do well in school) often portray gifted kids as threatened by indifferent schools that bore them, rather than challenging them and encouraging them to develop their gifts (Margolin 1994). Moreover, educational problems can be presented as threatening: How will America fare in a future when other nations' young workers are smarter and better educated than ours? In this view, there is nothing trivial about the Stupidity Epidemic; rather, it seems to pose a major threat to our national well-being.

Note that we need not assume that the critics who warn about the Stupidity Epidemic are cynical—individuals who know better but deliberately seek to scare people as a way to promote their issue. These advocates may be quite sincere. It is easy to get caught up in worrying about a social problem, to spend more and more time thinking about an issue and talking to other people who share that concern. Advocates often scare themselves before turning to the work of trying to frighten others.

Threatened Kids and a Precarious Future are Especially Scary

If scary claims grab people's attention, warnings about threatened children can be especially scary (Best 1990). We think of children as vulnerable, innocent, in need of protection. Children require care, help, and support; they cannot—and should not have to—care for themselves. Our society has all sorts of special arrangements designed to protect children: protective services to prevent child abuse; child labor laws to avoid economic exploitation; movie ratings designed to minimize exposure to images that might damage children; laws requiring that drivers place small children in approved safety seats; and on and on. These arrangements are designed to keep children safe from those who might hurt them, as well as from accidental harm. Such arrangements are the result of efforts of countless reformers who constructed various threats to children as social problems.

Obviously, the single most elaborate set of these child-centered arrangements are the schools. We have laws requiring that children attend school, that specify what they should study, that govern the qualifications of their teachers, and so on. We have these rules for two important reasons.

First, we believe that requiring that children receive schooling is essential for their own well-being. A child who isn't educated risks a lifetime of permanent poverty. Lower education has serious consequences: lower income, poorer health, shorter life expectancy, much greater risks of imprisonment, addiction, mental illness, and so on. Education is like a vaccination; it helps ward off potential problems and improves one's chances for a happier, healthier life. And, because we understand that children are vulnerable and dependent, and that they—and even their parents—may not make wise choices, we use the force of law to try and guarantee that children can benefit from school. As all children have no doubt been told at some point, educational arrangements are for their own good.

But there is a second reason to foster education: it is understood to be in society's best interest. There is a sense in which children are the walking, talking future; they are the next generation, what people like to describe as "our most important natural resource." Today's children will be tomorrow's scientists, doctors, inventors, and such;

we will depend upon them to make progress. Further, we suspect that they will need a good educational foundation to succeed, to face and overcome the future's challenges. We assume that the better educated a nation's citizens, the brighter that country's future. Educating the young will, then, benefit both the individuals who gain education, and the societies to which they belong.

These are fairly straightforward concerns: we need to do as much as we can to promote education because education offers direct, easily understood benefits. However, there is another side to making scary claims about children. Because children represent the future, worrying about kids becomes a way of addressing larger uncertainties about the future. We live at a time when there are lots of apocalyptic scenarios about future problems. What if there's a nuclear war? What it if is followed by a nuclear winter? What if there is an ecological catastrophe caused by some combination of overpopulation, resource depletion, and pollution? What if some new plague sweeps across the globe? Or maybe the global economy will collapse? Or the supervolcano beneath Yellowstone could explode, or a giant asteroid could strike earth. We hear lot of really scary claims about things that could happen, things that could end "life as we know it."

Most Americans are aware of at least some of these catastrophic concerns. And most of us sense that there is very little we can do as individuals to ward off any of these problems. It wouldn't be that hard to become paralyzed by worrying about the uncertain future. For some people, worrying about children (those proxies for the future) may be a way to transform fears into something more manageable. Devising arrangements to protect children—even minor improvements, such as requiring bicycle helmets and childproof caps on pill bottles—are a way of making the future a bit more secure. Therefore, when people proclaim that children are endangered, it doesn't matter whether the danger comes from child predators or failing schools—it is often possible to mobilize people to act, to take steps to protect children.

Fears about the Stupidity Epidemic, then, are compelling on several levels. We can worry about the lives of specific children who may be damaged by poor schooling, and about the risks this might pose to our nation's future, but it is also a way to transform unmanageable fears about future catastrophe into specific, practical things we can do to help the children who will populate the future.

Why Worry about the Stupidity Epidemic?

This section has offered six reasons why we are so fond of worrying about the Stupidity Epidemic. These reasons can be grouped into three categories. The first three reasons revolve around *plausibility*; that is, they suggest reasons why our everyday experience might lead us to conclude that we can see the effects of a Stupidity Epidemic: (1) the knowledge–ignorance paradox means that the amount of information people don't know is increasing, which suggests they may be getting dumber; (2) because our expectations for what students need to learn evolve, it is possible to point to things they no longer learn as evidence of a Stupidity Epidemic; and (3) as a growing proportion of students stay in high school or go on to college, the range of abilities among those students increases, making some of them seem less bright than their classmates. A second category of reasons concerns *convenience*: (4) blaming schools for failing to eliminate inequality provides a scapegoat for a broader set of social problems. Finally, presenting frightening claims is *effective*: (5) scaring people makes it easier to persuade them to act, and (6) scary claims about children are particularly effective because they tap into doubts about the future.

In other words, it is possible to understand why people worry about a Stupidity Epidemic. But aren't there better ways to think about educational issues?

DISCUSSION QUESTIONS

1. Explain the knowledge–ignorance paradox.
2. What are some examples of what schools consider essential knowledge changing over time?
3. Americans value equality, yet opinion polls suggest that they are not particularly troubled that there is inequality. Explain how their ideas about schools help reconcile these beliefs.
4. What does it mean to say that something is socially constructed? How can understanding the social construction of social problems help us think about the Stupidity Epidemic?

V: Beyond Stupidity

Better Ways to Think about Educational Issues

～～✕～～

At this point, it should be clear that fears of a Stupidity Epidemic are misplaced. Americans aren't getting dumber, and our schools aren't getting worse. But that doesn't mean that we shouldn't be concerned about the state of education. This final section suggests some better ways to think about educational issues.

To begin, we need to acknowledge that all the educational critics who have warned about the Stupidity Epidemic share an underlying—and correct—assumption: *education is indeed important*. Complex, modern societies demand a highly educated citizenry. My grandfathers may have been able to leave school after eighth grade and go on to build successful lives, but the prospects today for anyone leaving school at that age obviously are much less bright. Just think about all the jobs that require people to work with computers; those careers demand, not just literacy, but other complex reasoning skills. Increasingly, jobs—and especially jobs that pay well—require education. Moreover, education offers benefits beyond a higher income; more education is correlated with longer life expectancy, lower rates of all sorts of social problems, and so on. As a general rule, societies want as many people as possible to have as much education as possible: it is good for the educated individuals; and it is good for the society as a whole. The goals promoted by education reformers are valid: we would all benefit if more people received more schooling, if literacy skills improved, and so on.

Of course, *our schools can be improved*. No student can possibly learn everything, but it seems reasonable to believe that every student could learn more. This will be true for our best students, as well as our worst. There are lots of reformers with lots of ideas; these advocates represent all manner of positions and professions. Proposals for reform come from liberals and from conservatives, from students, parents, and teachers, from school administrators, educational researchers, and politicians, from journalists and members of particular ethnic and religious groups, and so on. These folks propose all sorts of ways of improving education. Some want to improve the way we teach the best students, and call for more and better gifted education programs, AP classes, and so on. Others want to help those students who have more difficulties with schooling by expanding programs to encourage prospective dropouts to stay in school, offering more and better remedial and special education classes, and so forth. Look at all of the proposals for improving education: smaller class sizes, higher teacher salaries, longer school years, more computers in classrooms, allowing students and their parents to choose their schools, and on and on. There are lots of ideas out there. And, because American education is organized around thousands of local school districts that set many of the policies for their schools, it is relatively easy for Americans to experiment, for a particular teacher, school, or school district to try out some new idea and see whether it works better than previous practices. Some reforms—not all, but some—prove to be successful, catch on, and begin to spread. Reform campaigns have been changing—and mostly improving—American education for two centuries, and we should welcome further improvements.

We also need to *specify what we want to improve.* One problem with talking about the Stupidity Epidemic is that it implies that everything is wrong, that nothing is working, that there's no solution in sight. This turns education into a single, possibly unmanageable social problem. Moreover, critics often insist that schools need to change in some particular way, that we need to encourage school choice, or have more standardized tests, or whatever. In other words, there are tendencies for both the diagnosis of the problem and the proposed solution to be simplistic. It is more useful to focus on particular issues.

Consider, for example, the pattern of ethnic differences in student performance, that is, that white students tend to remain in school longer than black and Hispanic students. This pattern has troubling implications: if nonwhites get less education, societal problems of ethnic inequality are more likely to continue into the future. How should we think about this specific issue?

One method that has been tried is to blame "failing schools," and to institute a system of standardized testing (mandated in the federal **No Child Left Behind Act [NCLB]** of 2001) as a means of pressuring schools to improve their teaching so that students of all ethnic groups achieved passing scores. In effect, NCLB not only held schools responsible for all differences in students' performance (a dubious, overly simplistic diagnosis of the problem), but further held that a standardized testing program could provide the necessary motivation for correcting the schools' flaws (an equally simplistic solution). Over the years, NCLB came in for a good deal of criticism for all sorts of reasons, which led to considerable disenchantment with the policy.

An alternative approach might be to recognize the way that ethnicity and social class are intertwined. The difficulties that nonwhite students have in school are less because they are nonwhite, than because larger proportions of them come from disadvantaged class backgrounds. We have already noted that Americans find it awkward to talk about class differences. But it is class, more than ethnicity, that shapes educational outcomes. Children raised in upper-middle-class homes are likely to have many advantages, including better educated parents who view school as especially important, and who can give their children a host of experiences and opportunities that improve their chances of doing well in school (Lareau 2003). This sort of enriched environment fosters good grades, which not only encourages staying in school, but opens all sorts of options for higher education, which in turn prepare those children to launch their own upper-middle-class lives.

In contrast, children from working- and lower-class homes are less likely to be groomed for success in school. They come from homes with adults who tend to be less educated than those in upper-middle-class families, and with fewer books, no or less powerful computers, less money to pay for activity fees and other special experiences, and so on. When people talk about the importance of education, it sometimes seems as though they are pretending that all students who enter kindergarten are equally well prepared for the school experience (or at least assuming that the school should be able turn all students into equally accomplished learners), and then blaming differences in students' performance on bad schools. This sort of talk ignores the reality of class differences, and attributing any differences in student performance to the schools' failure to teach well ignores all of the ways the world outside the classroom shapes students' behaviors. In other words, *education needs to be understood within its broader social context.*

We also need to appreciate that *social change is a process.* This is evident when we look at the history of American education. The historical record displays trends—more students getting more education, gaps between whites and nonwhites closing, and so on. It does not show sudden, overnight transformations. We should expect that the effects of any reform will be gradual, with modest improvement year after year.

Further, we need to appreciate that *education is an arena where people promote competing visions of the same values.* We like to think that our values—freedom, equality, justice, and the like—form a consistent, coherent whole, and that may be true when we think about values in their most abstract form. But values have to be operationalized; that is, people make specific proposals and call upon particular values to justify the causes they advocate. Consider equality. What does it mean to call for equal education? Does it mean that all children should be taught exactly the same lessons? What about children with learning disabilities—shouldn't they receive special help so that, at the end of the day, they have a more equal chance to learn? But what about gifted students? Don't they deserve special training so that they are challenged, so that all students have a equal opportunity to fulfill their potential? Does equality demand affirmative action policies to help make up for past injustices, or does it require that everyone receive exactly the same consideration? You get the idea. Even if everyone is in favor of equal education in principle, that hardly means they will agree on which educational policies support equality.

Precisely because people do worry about the welfare of their children, schools attract a lot of critical attention. Parents worry about whether the school is teaching what they want their children to learn: which explains why some folks choose to home-school their kids, or send them to parochial schools, or vote for school-board candidates who share their views on curriculum. Given the size of our country, and the economic and social diversity of its population, there will inevitably be many, many views about how schools ought to function, and about how education might be improved. This is inevitable; efforts to design one-size-fits-all educational programs are doomed. But this diversity and the decentralization of the educational system are also strengths, in that they foster innovation, in the form of local efforts to identify problems and devise reforms.

In short, thinking about educational issues requires that we locate students and schools in their broader social context. We need to appreciate the complexities of educational issues, rather than railing against a simplistic Stupidity Epidemic. Nor is education unique. There are lots of alarming claims about social problems. Claims about the Stupidity Epidemic have their counterparts in alarmist rhetoric about crime, immigration, and lots of other issues. Hopefully this chapter has helped you understand claims about the Stupidity Epidemic, but it should also give you some tools to think critically about other claims about social problems.

DISCUSSION QUESTIONS

1. Is there a difference between criticizing claims about the Stupidity Epidemic and saying that our existing schools are perfect? Explain.
2. The author argues that claims about the Stupidity Epidemic are too simplistic. In what ways does thinking about schools need to be more complex?

References

Arenson, Karen W. 2004. "Math and Science Tests Find 4th and 8th Graders in U.S. Still Lag Many Peers." *New York Times* (December 15): A29.

Bauerlein, Mark. 2008. *The Dumbest Generation: How the Digital Age Stupefies Young Americans and Jeopardizes Our Future.* New York: Tracher/Penguin.

Berliner, David C., and Bruce J. Biddle. 1995. *The Manufactured Crisis: Myths, Fraud, and the Attack on America's Public Schools.* Reading, MA: Addison-Wesley.

Best, Joel. 1990. *Threatened Children: Rhetoric and Concern about Child-Victims.* Chicago: University of Chicago Press.

———. 2001a. *Damned Lies and Statistics: Untangling Numbers from the Media, Politicians, and Activists.* Berkeley: University of California Press.

———. 2001b. "Social Progress and Social Problems: Toward a Sociology of Gloom." *Sociological Quarterly* 42: 1–12.

———. 2006. *Flavor of the Month: Why Smart People Fall for Fads.* Berkeley: University of California Press.

———. 2008. *Social Problems.* New York: Norton.

Blank, Grant. 2007. *Critics, Ratings, and Society: A Sociology of Reviews.* Lanham, MD: Rowman & Littlefield.

Boe, Erling E., and Sujie Shin. 2005. "Is the United States Really Losing the International Horse Race in Academic Achievement?" *Phi Delta Kappan* 86: 688–95.

Bracey, Gerald W. 2006. *Reading Educational Research: How to Avoid Getting Statistically Snookered.* Portsmouth, NH: Heinemann.

Briggs, Tracey Wong. 2007. "College Students Struggle on History Test," *USA Today Online* (September 19). Retrieved August 24, 2009 (www.usatoday.com).

Bronner, Ethan. 1998. "U.S. Trails the World in Math and Science: A Study of 12th Graders Prompts a Call for New Ways to Teach." *New York Times* (February 25): B10.

Celis, William, 3d. 1993. "Study Says Half of Adults in U.S. Lack Reading and Math Abilities." *New York Times* (September 9): A1.

Chaplin, Duncan. 2002. "Tassels on the Cheap." *Education Next* 2 (Fall): 24–29.

College Board. 2008. "SAT Scores Stable as Record Numbers Take Test." Press release, August 26. Retrieved April 10, 2010 (www.collegeboard.com).

Commission on the Skills of the American Workforce. 1990. *America's Choice: High Skills or Low Wages!* Rochester, NY: National Center on Education and the Economy.

Copperman, Paul. 1978. *The Literacy Hoax: The Decline of Reading, Writing, and Learning in the Public Schools and What We Can Do about It.* New York: Morrow.

Cremin, Lawrence A. 1990. *Popular Education and Its Discontents.* New York: Harper & Row.

D'Aimeé, Lys. 1900. "The Menace of Present Educational Methods." *Gunton's Magazine* 19: 257–67.

Davis, Fred. 1979. *Yearning for Yesterday: A Sociology of Nostalgia.* New York: Free Press.

Dean, Cornelia. 2005. "Scientific Savvy? In U.S., Not Much." *New York Times* (August 30): F3.

Delli Carpini, Michael X., and Scott Keeter. 1991. "Stability and Change in the U.S. Public's Knowledge of Politics." *Public Opinion Quarterly* 55: 583–612.

Dillon, Sam. 2008. "States' Inflated Data Obscure Epidemic of School Dropouts." *New York Times* (March 20): A1.

Fischer, Claude S., Michael Hout, Martín Sánchez Jankowski, Samuel R. Lucas, Ann Swidler, and Kim Voss. 1996. *Inequality by Design: Cracking the Bell Curve Myth.* Princeton, NJ: Princeton University Press.

Flesch, Rudolf. 1955. *Why Johnny Can't Read—and What You Can Do about It.* New York: Harper & Row.

———. 1985. "Why So Much Illiteracy?" *New York Times* (June 3): A19.

Flynn, James R. 2009. *What Is Intelligence?*, expanded ed. New York: Cambridge University Press.

Frank, Robert H. 2007. *Falling Behind: How Rising Inequality Harms the Middle Class.* Berkeley: University of California Press.

Gallup Poll. 2009. "Topics A to Z." Retrieved August 26, 2009 (www.gallup.com/poll/Topics.aspx?CSTS=wwwsitemap&to=POLL-Topics-A-to-Z).

Gatto, John Taylor. 2002. *Dumbing Us Down: The Hidden Curriculum of Compulsory Schooling,* 2nd edition. New York: New Society.

Goldin, Claudia (ed.). 2006. "Chapter Bc: Education." Pp. 2–387–498 in *Historical Statistics of the United States: Earliest Times to the Present,* Millennial edition. Volume Two, eds. Susan B. Carter, Scott Sigmund Gartner, Michael R. Haines, Alan L. Olmstead, Richard Sutch, and Gavin Wright. New York: Cambridge University Press.

Gonzales, Patrick, Trevor Williams, Leslie Jocelyn, Stephen Roey, David Kastberg, and Summer Brenwald. 2008. *Highlights from TIMSS 2007: Mathematics and Science Achievement of U.S. Fourth- and Eighth-Grade Students in an International Context* (NCES 2009–001 Revised). National Center for Education Statistics, Institute of Education Sciences, U.S. Department of Education. Washington.

Gorard, Stephen. 2001. "International Comparisons of School Effectiveness: The Second Component of the 'Crisis Account' in England?" *Comparative Education* 37: 279–96.

Griffiths, Rudyard. 2007. "Our Knowledge of Canada Is Falling with Every Poll." *Thestar.com* (July 2). Retrieved September 23, 2009 (www.thestar.com).

Gruson, Lindsey. 1986. "Widespread Illiteracy Burdens the Nation." *New York Times* (July 22): C1, C11.

Hampel, Robert L. 1986. *The Last Little Citadel: American High Schools Since 1940.* Boston: Houghton Mifflin.

Healy, Michelle. 2008. "U.S. Doesn't Know Civics." *USA Today* (November 20): 6D.

Henry, Julie. 2004. "Hitler Wasn't Real, Says One in 10 Historically Challenged Britons." *Sunday Telegraph* (London) (April 4): 5.

Herrnstein, Richard J., and Charles Murray. 1994. *The Bell Curve: Intelligence and Class Structure in American Life*. New York: Free Press.

Hess, Frederick M. 2008. *Still at Risk: What Students Don't Know, Even Now*. Washington: Common Core. Retrieved August 27, 2009 (www.commoncore.org).

Hilgartner, Stephen, and Charles L. Bosk. 1988. "The Rise and Fall of Social Problems." *American Journal of Sociology* 94: 53–78.

Hirsch, E. D., Jr. 2006. *The Knowledge Deficit: Closing the Shocking Education Gap for American Schoolchildren*. Boston: Houghton Mifflin.

Ipsos Reid. 2009. "Dominion Institute's New Canadian Icons Survey Reveals Some Not-So-Familiar Faces" (June 29). Retrieved September 23, 2009 (www.ipsos.ca).

Johnson, Steven. 2005. *Everything Bad Is Good for You: How Today's Popular Culture Is Actually Making Us Smarter*. New York: Riverhead.

Kaestle, Carl F. 1983. *Pillars of the Republic: Common Schools and American Society, 1780–1860*. New York: Hill and Wang.

Kozol, Jonathan. 1985. *Illiterate America*. New York: Plume.

Kutner, Mark, Elizabeth Greenberg, Ying Jin, Bridget Boyle, Yung-chen Hsu, and Eric Dunleavy. 2007. *Literacy in Everyday Life: Results from the 2003 National Assessment of Adult Literacy* (NCES 2007–480). U.S. Department of Education. Washington: National Center for Education Statistics.

Lareau, Annette. 2003. *Unequal Childhoods: Class, Race, and Family Life*. Berkeley: University of California Press.

Levy, Harold O. 2009. "Five Ways to Fix America's Schools." *New York Times* (June 8): 19.

Life. 1958. "Crisis in Education." (March 24): 26–35.

Margolin, Leslie. 1994. *Goodness Personified: The Emergence of Gifted Children*. Hawthorne, NY: Aldine de Gruyter.

National Center for Education Statistics (NCES). 2005. *Digest of Education Statistics: 2004*. Washington: U.S. Department of Education. Retrieved September 6, 2009 (http://nces.ed.gov/programs/digest/d04).

———. 2009. *NAEP 2008 Trends in Academic Progress*. Washington: U.S. Department of Education. Retrieved September 9, 2009 (http://nces.ed.gov/pubsearch/pubsinfo.asp?pubid=2009479).

———. 2010a. *Digest of Education Statistics: 2009*. Washington: U.S. Department of Education. Retrieved May 10, 2010 (http://nces.ed.gov/programs/digest/d09).

———. 2010b. "The Nation's Report Card: Long Term Trend." Retrieved April 8, 2010 (http://nationsreportcard.gov/ltt_2008).

National Commission on Excellence in Education. 1983. *A Nation at Risk: The Imperative for Educational Reform*. Washington: Department of Education. Retrieved August 28, 2009 (www.ed.gov/pubs/NatAtRisk/risk).

National Endowment for the Arts (NEA). 2004. *Reading at Risk: A Survey of Literary Reading in America*. Research Division Report #46. Washington: NEA.

———. 2007. *To Read or Not to Read: A Question of National Importance*. Washington: NEA.

———. 2008. *Reading on the Rise: A New Chapter in American Literacy*. Washington: NEA.

National Geographic–Roper Public Affairs. 2006. *2006 Geographic Literacy Study: Final Report*. Retrieved August 24, 2009 (http://www.nationalgeographic.com/roper2006/pdf/FINAL Report2006GeogLitsurvey.pdf).

National Science Board. 2010. *Science and Engineering Indicators 2010.* Arlington, VA: National Science Foundation (NSB 10–01).

New Commission on the Skills of the American Workforce. 2007. *Tough Choices or Tough Times: Executive Summary.* Washington: National Center on Education and the Economy. Retrieved August 27, 2009 (www.ncee.org).

New York Times. 1931a. "Van Dyke Champions Classics." (May 13): 18.

———. 1931b. "Yale Long Debated Dropping Classics." (May 13): 18.

———. 1986. "Study Says 5% of Young Adults Are Illiterate." (August 31): A28.

———. 1988. "Americans Falter on Geography Test." (July 28): A16.

Newspaper Association of America. 2010. "Trends and Numbers." Retrieved May 8, 2010 (http://www.naa.org).

Nichols, Lawrence T. 1995. "Cold Wars, Evil Empires, Treacherous Japanese: Effects of International Context on Problem Construction." Pp. 313–34 in *Images of Issues: Typifying Contemporary Social Problems,* 2nd ed., ed. Joel Best. Hawthorne, NY: Aldine de Gruyter.

Ogbu, John U., ed. 2008. *Minority Status, Oppositional Culture, and Schooling.* New York: Routledge.

O'Neill, Barry. 1994. "The History of a Hoax." *New York Times Magazine* (March 6): 46–49.

Packard, Frederick Adolpus. 1969 [1866]. *The Daily Public School in the United States.* New York: Arno.

Pew Research Center for The People and The Press. 2007. "Trends in Political Values and Core Attitudes." News release, March 22. Retrieved May 9, 2010 (http:people-press.org).

Powell, Brian, and Lala Carr Steelman. 1996. "Bewitched, Bothered, and Bewildering: The Use and Misuse of State SAT and ACT Scores." *Harvard Educational Review* 66: 27–59.

Ravitch, Diane. 2010. *The Death and Life of the Great American School System: How Testing and Choice Are Undermining Education.* New York: Basic.

Ravitch, Diane, and Chester E. Finn, Jr. 1987. *What Do Our 17-Year-Olds Know?* New York: Harper & Row.

Rickover, Hyman G. 1963. *American Education: A National Failure.* New York: Dutton.

Rinsland, Henry D. 1947. *A Basic Vocabulary of Elementary School Children.* New York: Macmillan.

Roper Center for Public Opinion Research. 2009. *iPOLL Databank.* Retrieved September 12, 2009 (http://roperweb.ropercenter.uconn.edu).

Sadler, Michael E. 1903. "Impressions of American Education." *Educational Review* 25: 217–31.

Schemo, Diana Jean. 2000. "Worldwide Survey Finds U.S. Students Are Not Keeping Up." *New York Times* (December 6): A1, A22.

Shenkman, Rick. 2008. *Just How Stupid Are We? Facing the Truth about the American Voter.* New York: Basic.

Silberman, Charles E. 1970. *Crisis in the Classroom: The Remaking of American Education.* New York: Random House.

Smith, Carl B., and Gary M. Ingersoll. 1984. *Written Vocabulary of Elementary School Pupils, Ages 6–14.* Monograph in Language and Reading Studies 6. Bloomington, IN: Indiana University School of Education.

Stanley, Jane. 2010. *The Rhetoric of Remediation: Negotiating Entitlement and Access to Higher Education.* Pittsburgh: University of Pittsburgh Press.

Takayama, Keita. 2007. "*A Nation at Risk* Crosses the Pacific: Transnational Borrowing of the U.S. Crisis Discourse in the Debate on Education Reform in Japan." *Comparative Education Review* 51: 432–46.

Trent, James W., Jr. 1994. *Inventing the Feeble Mind: A History of Mental Retardation in the United States.* Berkeley: University of California Press.

Ungar, Sheldon. 2003. "Misplaced Metaphor: A Critical Analysis of the 'Knowledge Society'." *Canadian Review of Sociology and Anthropology* 40: 331–47.

———. 2008. "Ignorance as an Under-Identified Social Problem." *British Journal of Sociology* 59: 301–26.

U.S. News and World Report. 1956. "We Are Less Educated than 50 Years Ago." (November 30): 68–47, 79–80, 82.

Veblen, Thorstein. 1953 [1899]. *The Theory of the Leisure Class: An Economic Study of Institutions.* New York: New American Library.

Walsh, Mary. 2005. "Survey Finds Many Have Poor Grasp of Basic Economics," *New York Times* (April 27): C3.

Werner, Leslie Maitland. 1986. "13% of U.S. Adults Are Illiterate in English, a Federal Study Finds." *New York Times* (April 21): A1.

Glossary/Index

functional literacy: the ability to read and write at some specified level (e.g., a third-grade level), sufficient to comprehend a particular set of practical texts (e.g., understanding directions for preparing for a medical test) 23–24

G

Gallup Poll (see public opinion polls)

General Educational Development (GED): certification of having completed the equivalent of high school 11–12, 15–16

gifted children 37

graduate education 14

Great Britain, concerns about education 2-3

H

high school graduation 10–12, 15–16

I

ignorance 30–31

illiteracy 23

inequality 35–36

international rivals 5–6

IQ (intelligence quotient) tests: standardized tests designed to measure an individual's intelligence 26–28

J

Japan

   concerns about education 3

   rival to U.S. 5

K

knowledge society: a society that generates a large amount of new information 30

knowledge–ignorance paradox (KIP): as societal knowledge expands, ignorance increases because individuals command an increasingly smaller share of all knowledge 30–31

L

literacy: traditionally, the ability to read or write, but often used in reference to particular sorts of knowledge (e.g., geographic literacy) or particular levels of intellectual skill (e.g., functional literacy) (see also functional literacy, illiteracy)

   civic 21–22

   geographic 1

   scientific 21–22

V

values 43
VCR: video cassette recording 33
vocabularies, schoolchildrens' 25–26

W

workforce: a country's working population, referring to both the people and their skills 4–5

Made in the USA
Monee, IL
20 January 2020